Encouraging Words

Murray was one of the most influential leaders in my career. He was like a father figure to me—someone I grew up with—someone I knew would always be there. He was someone that would push and challenge me. Murray has the biggest heart but also some of the biggest expectations for his leaders. He could encourage an entire team with one of his signature morning meetings but also built a culture where expectations were crystal clear. Murray believed in me before I believed in myself. He saw something in me and found such opportunities for me to grow. I never fully understood those opportunities initially (like going overnight two weeks after getting married), but I trusted him and now looking back, those experiences are some of the richest I've had in my career. When self-doubt would continue to sneak in, "Do I have what it takes?" Murray was always there, believing in me.

He was my cheerleader, sounding board, and truth teller. I still have a note from Murray when I left T1375 the second time, a note I've often read when I've felt that doubt coming in—the fear of failure. His words still encourage me today in a different company and a different role.

So, Murray, thank you for believing in a twenty-two-year-old nearly fifteen years ago. You helped me see what I could be and you'll always be "one of the very best" to me. Forever grateful.

— Anne Marie Persico

Murray, first of all, thank you for inviting me to join your T1375 team back in 2016. I know my time shared with you is a small speckle in the time you were with Target, but in that short time you created a huge impact in my life in so many ways. I couldn't have asked for a better leader than you, and you're one of the genuine leaders out there who paves the way to make those around them better. You've been a great mentor and made me a better leader. You inspired me to be better each day and overcome my limits. You challenged me every day and sometimes drove me bonkers, but I wouldn't have it any other way. You uncovered a side of me that made me a stronger and more confident leader. I appreciate you truly believing in me when I didn't.

I have become who I am today because of you, and I'll be forever grateful to have spent this time with you. Thank you for always giving me the courage I needed and believing in me when no one else did. You told me to be who I am and not change for anyone—I really appreciate that. Thank you for everything. Thank you for showing me how to be a true leader—one that inspires their team to be better, challenge their limits, overcome their obstacles, and accomplish their goals. Perfect is good enough!

— Nicole Becker

Dearest Murray, you, my friend, are a game-changer. It's been five years since I've worked for you, and I still go back to the days when you helped shape me and develop me in my early years. You brought out confidence, empowerment, hard work, and loyalty in me—those traits have been foundational in my work and family life today. Another thing I love about you is that you're genuine to who you are and how you operate. Your humor, laugh, and fun-loving spirit made coming into the store not "work," but more like a family! I will be forever grateful I worked for you and grew alongside you in life. I appreciate how you've continued to mentor me over the years, and I want nothing more than for that to continue.

— Jessie Witt

Your Time to Shine

In Leadership and Life

Murray Williams

STREAMLINE BOOKS

To Jessie: You're amazing! Thank you for being my partner, the love of my life, my biggest supporter, and a wonderful mom and stepmom to our kids. I love you more each day and look forward to what the future holds for us!

(Murray, Jessie, Kyle, Jackie, Sara, Jake, and Josh)

To Josh: You're an intelligent, talented person and a free spirit. I love you! I'm so proud of you for serving our country and the person you've become. Each new day is a gift, and I look forward to what is ahead for you.

To Jake: I love you! You continue to prove that you can do whatever you put your mind to and succeed. I'm so proud of you. You're a great son, husband, and dad, and I'm so happy for the life you're building with Sara. Thank you for making us grandparents for the first time—we love Aurora so much!

To Kyle: I love you! You're a terrific bonus son and one of the best humans I know. Now is your time to shine as you build your life with Jackie. You have all the tools you need to have an amazing life, Kyle. I'm so proud of all you've accomplished so far, and I'm excited to watch you soar in the future.

Contents

Section Five

Never Stop Learning
The Rest of the Story

Initial Message

Thanks for taking a chance on me by purchasing my first book. Mine is likely different from other self-help or leadership books you've read. Rather than picking up a book and reading with little knowledge about the author, my desire is for you to get to know me differently. I think gaining additional perspective about my story will add credibility to the point of view shared throughout the book. I hope it does!

Buckle up as I spend some extra time on my story and the moments in my life that shaped me and how I lead. After that, we'll get deeper into the good stuff.

Again, thank you!

Murray

Foreword

A poem by Nick Hanson, an executive on my team many years ago, written when I retired:

My favorite, Murray
He would show up to the store
with a fire in his eye
Motivating his team
to reach for the sky
Blood, sweat and tears
from the team working overnight
All the visit prep and set walks
needed to be just right
The passion overflowed
with sweat running down his face
If you really messed up
he would put you in your place
What I will remember most

is how much that he cared
About your career, your family,
and anything you shared
He would develop you, coach you,
and put you to the test
His focus was to help you,
to challenge you to be your very best
A leader that you trust
and for you he would go to bat
Once you worked there you were family
and I was so thankful for that
He made work fun, he was quirky
and always celebrated his team
He picked you up, dusted you off
and got you focused on your dream
I will end this poem with a quote
which I think fits how many feel
What I loved most about Murray
was that he was . . . real

My Story

The leadership message I have to share is rooted in my personal story, so allow me to take you through my sixty-plus years and counting . . .

I'm from a large family, number six of eight kids, all of whom have names starting with "M": Mark, Mona, Mindy, Mickey, Mary, Murray, Meg, and Matt, in that order. My mom, Marie, sometimes regretted naming us as they did, especially when disciplining and working to quickly find the correct name. There are only 12 years between the youngest and oldest kids. We took an entire pew at St. Raphael's Catholic Church every Sunday!

My dad, Paul, had the "easy" job of paying the bills while mom ran the house and, in many ways, raised us—eight very unique kids. Mark (retired now) was a trained Navy pilot and chief purser officer on ships. After the military, he was the chief internal auditor for the Port of New Orleans. Mona and Mary spent their work years shaping our county's youth and future as teachers; both are retired. Mindy was a highly successful lead project manager. Mickey had his own business and is currently an IT professional for one of the largest companies in the world. Meg retired as a VP at Target Corporation, and Matt owns a successful business.

We were raised in the same three-bedroom rambler in Crystal, a suburb of Minneapolis, Minnesota (The Land of 10,000 Lakes). As our family grew, dad built a separate garage and remodeled our old one into a large bedroom that I shared with two of my brothers. The room was cold in the winter, so mom always put several extra blankets on the beds. She'd add so many that their weight prevented us from moving much, which helped when I was sharing a double bed with my brother Mick.

I don't know how my parents managed to provide for all of us in the early years. Mom used to say if we had a roof over our heads, food on the table, and faith in our hearts, we would be just fine. She was right.

My parents had firm values, especially about faith, family, and doing the right thing. Mom lived her faith daily and practiced what she preached, putting her feet on the ground for what she believed. For example, she spent hours walking and praying in front of an abortion clinic in bitterly cold weather, to the point that she had severe frostbite and almost lost several toes. My sister Mindy proclaimed years ago at a family event that our family was indeed "normal." Whatever. You can be the judge, I guess.

Dad was a quiet and reflective man and the sales manager at a lumber company for forty-plus years. He also had a fantastic talent for woodworking. Several of us boys share the affection for working with wood, and we all have dad-made things in our homes today. It warms my heart that my son, Jake, is following in my dad's footsteps with the same hobby. Every time he creates something, those memories of my dad are closer.

Dad's talents extended to carpentry as he built his parents' house—now our family lake place. He also built a cabin that was a prize at our church festival. He used to lead these large, multifaceted festivals over the years (mom was also involved, but in other ways). I can still remember how he interacted with people. He always seemed to be having fun. At the time, I had no idea how hard that sort of thing could be, especially with an all-volunteer workforce. What I recall seeing him do through other people was incredible.

Dad was also the grocery shopper and knew

where the deals were. He instilled in me that "you get what you pay for." In other words, you're better off buying the best with some things when they're made better and last much longer. If you were born in the '6os and early '7os, you might remember Bumper tennis shoes. They were the hottest thing. There were fake, less expensive versions and the real, official ones. Unfortunately, Dad never felt those shoes merited buying the best, so we had the cheaper model.

Throughout my life, especially after being blessed with kids, I have often thought about how I was raised and precisely what impacted how I matured. I haven't pinpointed one or two, or even a few specific things, and have since concluded that it's a sum-total thing.

While I can't remember which parent was directly involved, I clearly recall an early lesson about having a firm handshake when meeting some-one. We practiced it as kids. We were encouraged to look the person square in the eye and offer a firm, confident handshake and a smile. I am often reminded of that lesson, especially when I meet someone who never learned that, as it has served me well.

A firm handshake, solid eye contact, and a smile make all the difference when meeting people.

Mom . . . Well, she was AMAZING.

She was raised on a farm with her ten siblings (cheap farm labor, she used to say). She was a fantastic cook and prepared whatever we wanted for breakfast each morning, plus a rotating menu of home-cooked goodness the rest of the week. She enforced the firm rule of eating supper as a family every night, and I don't remember anyone missing more than a few of those dinners.

All of us kids became adept farmers as we each had jobs maintaining a small piece of land on granny's farm, providing most of the vegetables and fruit we ate. Mom and my sisters canned or froze everything—we had a large fruit cellar and an extra freezer in the basement. She was also a talented seamstress who made many of the clothes we wore when we were young. All the sisters learned those same skills in the kitchen and with a sewing machine from mom. She was a great teacher and a better listener. Her kids were her Joy!

When we were young we would take family outings to Duluth to pick rocks from the shore of

Lake Superior—large buckets of rocks—trailer fulls! The waves from Lake Superior made the rocks smooth and round and great for painting. She would paint phrases or quotes on them (calligraphy was also something she enjoyed), then she and my dad would go to craft fairs on weekends to sell them, along with all sorts of wooden goodies that he had made. She took orders if folks wanted different phrases, which happened frequently.

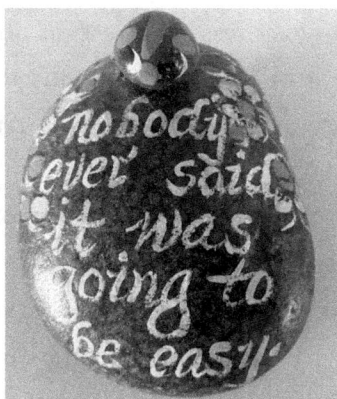

A rock from my shelf that mom painted. If the rock was bigger, it would have included "Enjoy the Journey."

Mom was always reading and taking classes to learn more about anything she found interesting. One of these topics was flowers. She made incredible flower arrangements and did all the flowers for my sisters' weddings, as well as other weddings and events. In her later years, she showed me how to create flower arrangements, and I still have the centerpiece we created together.

My parents were a great team and complemented each other well. I played soccer throughout school, including college, and I don't remember my parents ever missing a game. My siblings would say the same regarding their activities.

If you'd believe it, I haven't even touched on the real magic of my mom yet. Throughout our lives, she met every one of us where we were and tailored her teaching specifically to each of us. She made us feel like we were the most important thing in her life, encouraged us to be who we were, and always found a way to be supportive, even if she disagreed with the subject. Her support, guidance, and teachings made me who I am. While I don't remember the context, the expectation to always do your best came through loud and clear. I recall her saying when I was very young that if you always worked hard and did your best, you could do whatever you wanted to do and be whatever you wanted to be. Again, she was right. She and my dad were definitely "glass half full" people and encouraged the same from each of us. Hard work, doing your best, and a positive attitude were the keys to everything.

When mom turned eighty, Mindy helped us

create "The Eighty Reasons We Love You," a memory box to which everyone added their thoughts. Here's one of my favorites: "She showed us the beauty in simple things like weeds, rocks, freshly sliced tomatoes, a neatly stacked woodpile, and a new idea. She taught us that 'the best things in life aren't things.'"

My parents were lucky enough to die in their beds with family around them, and Meg gave the eulogy at mom's funeral. I wanted to include these words from what she shared:

Our mom was one strong woman or, as she would say, "one tough farmer." We love and admire her faith and respect for life, her strength and family values, and her sense of style (classic styles often accessorized with a great scarf), her many artistic talents, her self-sufficiency & independence (better known as stubbornness), her love of learning new things, and her love of taking care of us. We'll try to live by some of your favorite words and phrases like "Offer it up," "Smell the fresh country air," "Drink your milk," "Make your bed," and "Trust the good in others." And, of course, there are her classic lines, "Fox smells his own hole first," and "They won't buy the cow if you give the milk for free." Those obviously celebrate the farmer in her!

Mom lived twenty-plus years longer than dad,

and as a tough old farmer, I remember her telling me that she wanted to "die with her boots on." That's how she lived, always on the move and helping people. The stories she told.

She lived well into her nineties and needed more hands-on care in her home for the last few years. We were fortunate that seven of the eight kids live nearby, so we each took a night and a day every week to be with her. It was simply the best time with her; I have many memories, photos, and videos from those years. Thank God for technology and the opportunity to spend that time with her! I was always mom's favorite, often reminding her and my siblings of that fact. She insisted that she loved everyone the same, but I know better.

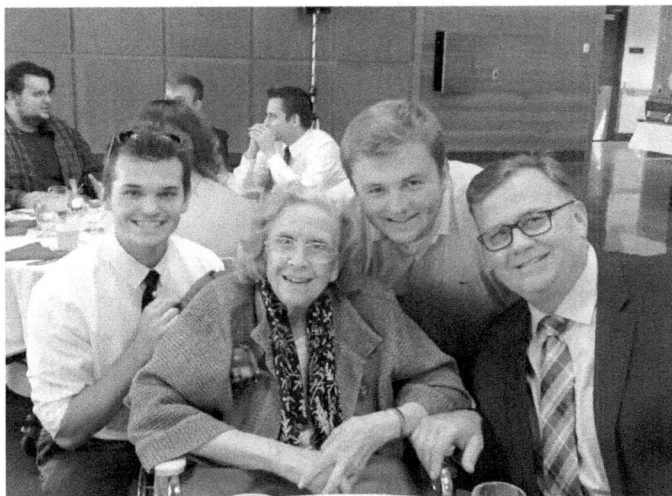

Some important people in my life: Jake, Mom, and Kyle at a family wedding a few years ago.

My parents have both passed, but all of us kids were fortunate to call those two Mom and Dad. It was clear they lived their lives entirely for their family. They challenged us with high expectations and set lofty standards. Everything was focused on keeping faith, family, and others first.

Some say that you are the combination of nature, nurture, and a bunch of life experiences. They say that a strong foundation built at home significantly impacts how things go later in life. While I know that everyone has amazing life stories to share, it was undoubtedly true for me. I am the product of two great parents, a wonderful family and great people around me, plus many life and work experiences.

I encourage you to spend some time reflecting on your journey, leadership and otherwise, and those situations that had the most significant impact on you—positive and negative. Why were they the most impactful, and what did you learn? Would those around you benefit from you sharing them?

My career has involved leading teams of all sizes with two of the largest retailers in the United States, the last 31 years at Target. However, it all started with curtains, critters, and TV dinners.

My First Place

After graduating from college, I took a job as a management trainee in a small town about an hour from home in New Ulm, Minnesota. I was officially on my own without the direct influence and problem-solving guidance of my parents and siblings, and I had significant anxiety about it. The only place available in my price range was the top floor of an old house with unstable, rickety exterior steps. It had one bedroom, a tiny living room, and an even smaller kitchen. The bathroom was crammed into the old, long, skinny stairwell space. My starting salary was around eleven thousand a year, and it was tough to make ends meet. I learned to love Swanson's TV dinners (which my folks would have ready when I went home every other weekend), Salisbury Steak was my preferred choice, and Malt-O-Meal my favorite breakfast.

Times were different then. Everything was new to me, and I was lonely. I didn't have a TV and wanted a stereo to listen to music, but I couldn't afford it. I went to the local bank to ask for a loan with no money or previous credit and was turned down twice. The next day I went back and asked to speak to the bank manager. He, too, said no. I firmly asked him how someone like myself, a new college graduate with a starting job, could establish credit if no one gave them a chance. After some additional discussion, he agreed to provide me with the $350 loan I needed for the stereo system I wanted, saying, "If you don't make your loan payments, I myself will hunt you down!"

That moment is something I'll never forget, and it helped shape my perspective going forward. It was the earliest I could recall standing on my own two feet and fighting for myself, and I felt great about it. Through moments like that, as I experienced each new situation and struggle and worked through it, I realized I had the confidence and persistence to make it on my own. It was a precious lesson, and I vowed to myself then and there that if I were ever in a situation where someone was asking me for a chance, I would give them the opportunity if I could.

Curtains and Critters

The winters were cold, and I don't think there was any insulation in that old house. Thankfully, utilities were included, but the furnace couldn't keep up. When the wind blew, the curtains would swing like the window was open, so I'd hang a blanket over each window. Like in my childhood bedroom, I survived by adding layers of covers to my bed and taking quick

showers. I remember one winter night was exceptionally frigid—a cold drink left on the window ledge in
my bedroom iced over. I tried creating my own insulation by wadding up newspaper and filling the space
between the window glass and screens. It slowed the
curtains from moving but eliminated virtually all
natural light. Those nights, when the temperature
reached negative thirty, I'd set my alarm every two
hours and venture down the crappy steps. In the
cold, I'd let my car run until it was warm so it would
start the following morning for my shift as opening
manager.

I realized I wasn't alone in that house early on,
possibly the first night. As I lay in bed, I could hear
mice running in the walls and the attic, and I listened
to what sounded like birds' wings fluttering. I learned
later that there were bats in the attic. The next day, I
set about a dozen mouse traps and would routinely
get two or three munchers per night for several
weeks.

Before those New Ulm days, I would let one of
the older siblings handle any mouse situations we
may have had at home. Except once. I looked out the
basement door on a frigid winter day and saw a
mouse a few feet from the door on the patio. I
grabbed the broom, went out, and aggressively
smacked it. I hit it so many times and so hard that I

snapped the weathered red broom handle. Mom was in the basement working on her crafts, saw the commotion, and came over to check things out. I'm smiling as I recall when she said, "You got it good, Murr!" as she reached down to pick it up, realizing it was frozen solid. Later, in my own place, I couldn't rely on my family's assistance and encouragement to take care of things. Those early work years were an exciting and often challenging start for my career, but I remember them fondly.

My initial work-related leadership experience was in retail stores where I learned the basics of running the operation and leading teams. From there, time spent in several different roles (district, regional office, and headquarters) exposed me to a wide variety of leaders and environments. It became apparent that while the roles and situations were very different, the ingredients needed for successful leadership were virtually the same.

Throughout my career, each new challenge provided me an opportunity to grow. Even when I struggled, especially when I struggled, those situations provided me with many moments of learning and inspiration. Those experiences, along with the opportunity to work with and observe many talented people, impacted me greatly and helped form a strong base for the leader I was to become. I learned to always err on the people's side, giving struggling folks one more chance than my boss or others thought appropriate. That patience and belief in each individual served me well over the years.

> Trust in others. Always err on the people's side, giving them ample opportunities to improve and grow.

As I was evaluating the timing around my decision to enter this new season in my career beyond my direct leadership roles, one factor that inspired me was all the change in our world. Included in those changes is a sort of "leadership evolution" in my view. Now more than ever there's a need for leaders to constantly connect, learn, and adjust. Coronavirus heightened the challenge to effective leadership as the world adjusted to increased remote work, to name just one change we've seen.

I'm all about leadership, so the topics I cover here have that focus. However, my ultimate goal is to inspire beyond leadership. I saved everything and anything that positively impacted me and my desire to be my best throughout my career. I realized early on I wanted to share what I was learning to help inspire others on their path. This book is my next step in that process. I hope getting to know me and my story sparked interest in my leadership journey. I encourage you to believe that *everything you need to find success is already within you,* you just need to recognize it, refine it, and grow it.

Are you still with me? Is that enough Murr-history? I'm guessing yes, so let's get started.

Memories and Moments:

Your Time to Shine

Introduction

What is **LEADERSHIP?**

Too often, people confuse management with leadership, but there's a significant difference.

People who refer to themselves as leaders are generally operating as managers the majority of the time. Management is *the process* of controlling things or people. In contrast, leadership is *the art* of motivating people to accomplish a common goal.

Authentic leadership goes well beyond that. Here are a couple of my favorite perspectives regarding management versus leadership:

"Management is about persuading people to do things that they do not want to do, while leadership is about inspiring people to do what they didn't think they could."

— Steve Jobs, Co-Founder and CEO of Apple

"A leader is someone who takes on the responsibility for and holds themselves accountable for finding the potential in others and encouraging the development of that potential." [1]

— Brené Brown, Author, Speaker, and Professor

The best definition of leadership is a combination of the two. It includes character and connection, encouraging and inspiring, development and investment. It's about putting the mission and the individuals on your team ahead of yourself.

Depending on your source, more than thirty thousand leadership books are available. I'm sure many believe the world doesn't need another, but I'm not one of those people. We each bring unique skills and experiences to define how we lead and inspire others.

The challenge as a leader is continuously growing and refining your leadership style and skills to maximize your impact on those you lead. As I see it, as long as you lead with integrity, there's no right or wrong way to approach things but rather degrees of leadership success.

Many new leaders think they should be the CEO in short order and search for whatever shortcuts to success they can find. Unlike baby boomers or Generation X, millennials and Generation Z don't necessarily see "climbing the career ladder" as the main goal. While pay is a factor, they want mentorship, connection, and significant relationships. They don't have the same attachment or loyalty to their place of employment that my generation had. They want time and attention and to be part of groups with shared interests, similar motivation, and a winning mentality. They're looking for inspiration, not just direction. That said, no matter how you slice it, there's still a strong need for hard work and focused effort to succeed. Leadership can be as complicated or simple as you want to make it, and for me, simplicity works best in almost all cases.

As the leader, you set the tone and, as I like to say, "define the curbs" for your team. In addition, you determine and keep the environment and culture. People need varying levels of guidance and coaching due to their experience and expertise, so the "curbs" on their road to success get more spread out as they grow and develop (since they require less structure and guidance). Without defined curbs, new leaders sometimes struggle to see a clear path forward. This can impact their early success and, as a result, their confidence to push through challenges. Every leader's primary responsibility is to bring out the best in others and inspire them on their path. Hopefully, that path is one of continuous improvement, enabling them to soar with their strengths and consistently move toward realizing their full potential. Contributing to and watching that growth happen has been the greatest reward in my career.

You'll see the topics I discuss aren't new. As I mentioned, when talking about a topic as broad as leadership, there is much to gain by keeping it simple.

The best interpretation of leadership is around connecting the heart. L-O-V-E.

L: Love, Learning, Laughter, and Luck
O: Ownership, Openness, and Optimism
V: Vulnerability, Vision, and Volition
E: Energize and Empathy

I hope this combination of ingredients will be as

successful for you as I found them. L-O-V-E is the path; how you define it is up to you.

What follows is my recipe for leadership success.

Section One
Invest in Your People

"They may not remember what you said or did—but they will never forget how you made them feel."

— Carl W. Buehner

Chapter 1
Love

When it comes to leadership, I want to highlight these four key "L" ingredients: Love, Learning, Laughter, and Luck.

The relationships you form are essential as they'll support you throughout your career. They'll also, in many ways, determine your success as a leader. You've likely heard that people don't leave their jobs, they leave their bosses. A solid foundation formed by a genuine supervisor relationship is the key to connecting and inspiring your team *and* to retaining them. In addition, the social connections formed are why you often hear folks say "the people" when asked what they miss most after leaving. I found myself saying that same thing when I retired.

The *starting point* for outstanding leadership is genuine affection (love) for everyone on your team.

Each individual needs to know you care about them and value what they bring. They also need to feel your positive expectations and confidence in them, and they should know you're committed to helping them grow toward their full potential. Several of the notes I received as I left Target shared this theme. For example, "He challenged me to be the best person I could be and believed in me more than I did myself. I've never felt as supported as I did when working for Murray." There is no greater compliment for a leader than that. Trust me, I benefited greatly from working with each of them.

> *"Coach me, and I will learn. Push and challenge me, and I will grow. Believe in me, and I will win."*

> — Dr. Robert Halgren

Love doesn't happen without trust, which means your folks know you support them and have their back no matter what. It can't be a conditional support, but visible, consistent, unwavering belief in them. It's like raising kids— my team members are my extended family. I want what's best for them and encourage them to do their best.

Growth, development, and future success are likely if you've established mutual trust. Trust forms by getting to know each person, personally and professionally, and learning his or her strengths and interests. Being genuine in building those individual relationships is crucial and foundational. Be genuinely interested in your people and ask clarifying, understanding questions. Listen to what they share, ask them how to help when appropriate, and note those conversational "nuggets" to remember and refer to later.

A friend recently shared that she had planned a memorable trip home to visit her mom who was having health issues. Despite talking about her mom and taking the trip, her supervisor never bothered to ask about her mom or how my friend was doing. What a missed opportunity! While she liked and respected her supervisor, I know that bothered her.

> Great leaders genuinely care about their people and show it often.

During my initial meeting with Libby, a leader who was early in her career, she talked about her family of four. She had such great love for her family, especially her brother who had special needs. Pride was oozing out of her as she shared her story. She told me about her brother's joy for life and his unconditional love, among other things. Many stories were shared throughout our years working together, and I know that initial conversation laid the foundation for a relationship that still exists today.

Libby was *the person* on our team—the glue everyone loved and rallied around. She was rock solid and crucial to our team's success during challenging times. Unsurprisingly, I still saw pictures of her on the desks and screensavers of people she led many years after moving on to her next role.

In addition to a personal connection, encouraging each person in their careers is crucial. Even the newest members should have successes that move them forward. All members need to feel they positively impact the team. Recognizing and acknowledging contributions is vital.

> Meet each person where they are in their development. Remember the importance of encouraging progress and recognizing contributions.

Every person on your team is essential. Your responsibility as a leader revolves around establishing that initial relationship and then investing in them as it grows.

Show Visible Support

I had the incredible opportunity and honor to lead the team at Target's flagship store, located directly across the street from the corporate headquarters. It's a high-traffic, multi-level store where we tested new initiatives for the company. Many of those initiatives contributed directly to the company's expansion into metro markets in recent years, with smaller-sized stores driving the company's growth today.

Using my parents' "glass half full" viewpoint, always trying to keep our challenges viewed through a positive lens, I often told my team and others that we had twelve thousand experts at HQ helping us run the store daily. That always made it interesting, to say the least.

Since we were located right across the street from HQ, we were often challenged to do what the company referred to as "early sets," meaning we would set transitioning areas a couple of weeks before the rest of the chain did. Those sets always involved significantly more work. The goal was to discover any misses or issues with the set direction to develop better solutions for the rest of the stores. The HQ team would walk the store . . .

One season, my team had worked a mini-miracle by executing an exceptionally challenging and complicated holiday set, including capturing detailed notes for the HQ team to resolve. Every issue was addressed and documented by my team before the walk.

A group of around twenty people from HQ had just completed the walk-through, and some lingered after. One picked up a bag of gutter clips for Christmas lights, which we'd discovered had poor packaging. When the person picked up the bag, it opened and a hundred gutter clips spewed all over the floor. As he reached down to pick them up, the other said, "Stop. You don't have to do that, that's their job," pointing at some of my team members nearby. They nodded agreement, chuckled condescendingly, and walked away, leaving the clips all over the floor.

On the surface, picking up gutter clips may not seem like a big deal, but knowing how hard my team had worked on this set and the fact that we were under constant scrutiny daily, it was vital for me to do something when I was informed of the incident.

I identified the highest level person who attended the walk that morning and gave him a call. As you would hope, he was infuriated by what he heard. A few minutes later, he called me back, saying he would send those responsible to apologize to my team. He also assured me that he'd do what was necessary to prevent anything like this from happening again. That situation permanently changed how our teams interacted. Later that week, several from my team and a few key HQ partners met and established a visit protocol—a partnership if you will—for all future visits. The protocol included always having my team participate and provide timely feedback.

Because I supported and advocated for my team, change was able to take place that improved the relationship and efficiency of the way we worked together going forward.

Leadership Tip

Periodically, I'll share some leadership must-haves, such as what I call *maintaining professional distance.* One of the most frequent mistakes leaders make, experienced and inexperienced, is not keeping that "professional distance." As a leader, your role is to introduce your team to future possibilities, and your mission is to inspire them to set goals to improve each day. Maintaining clarity around your leadership role is crucial, as is ensuring no overlap between business activities and after-work, leisure activities. In a nutshell, you can't be their leader and drinking buddy. The career impact on both people involved and, often, the team, will be devastating.

Lean into Courageous Conversations

Just like parents and their kids, there are times when leaders need to employ more direct encouragement, which I like to refer to as "tough love." Sometimes, your coaching and guidance as a leader just aren't working for whatever reason. Frequently, less experienced leaders feel uncomfortable using tough love when it's needed. If your team members aren't performing well, it could erode your entire team's culture and continuity. That can be hard to repair.

You're only as good as your weakest link. As a leader, your team must know if you have concerns about their performance, as they deserve the opportunity to address them. People can't fix things if they're unaware of the issues. Since most leaders want to be liked and respected, it's helpful to remember that it's not the person you have problems with, but their behavior.

> Treat people respectfully and in a manner that you want to be treated. Always stick up for yourself and your team when needed. Build a trusted foundation with honest feedback.

In my experience, the time you spend preparing for those more challenging conversations will pay off tenfold (and that prep will ease your anxiety). During those conversations, practice being comfortable with silence—pause to allow your team member to hear and absorb the discussion. The key to success in this area is to prepare well and always come from a place of honesty, support, and investment.

Chapter 2
Learning

One of the life lessons I learned from my parents is always do your best—anything less is wasted effort. That fueled my desire for continuous learning.

Always be curious, ask questions to learn, and don't be afraid to make mistakes. Take time to reflect on what you have learned and know, practice it, and make necessary adjustments. I always have a small notebook in my pocket so I can write down ideas. It's also helpful to have one on your nightstand—being able to "park" your thoughts will probably help you get some rest. Along the same lines, I always encourage folks to ask questions when they have them or write them down to ensure you get them answered ASAP. There are no dumb questions other

than those that didn't get asked, so always be courageous and ask them.

> Jot down ideas in a notebook. "Park" your
> thoughts for later. Ask questions to gain a better
> understanding.

Are you an Athlete?

There are benefits to thinking about your career like
a star athlete. Athletes are usually the hardest workers, relentlessly practicing and constantly looking to
refine and develop new skills. They enlist the
support of others (physical trainers, training buddies,
sports psychologists, etc.), and often seek advice from
experienced friends and successful people to guide
them. The same is true for successful leaders.
They're constantly looking to better themselves and
have their team, including peers and mentors, to
help.

Like great athletes, the more you stay in "rookie
mode" from a learning perspective, the more
successful you'll become. Dig in, do the hard work,
and do whatever's necessary to move forward.

When I was about to start my first leadership
position in Williston, North Dakota, I memorized the

different retail department numbers and the average gross margins in those departments (more than sixty of them). In addition, I learned all the unique company terms and the story of how the store came to be. Many thought I was way over the top, but it helped me get off to a good start even just from a confidence standpoint. In addition, one of the best things I did for myself early on was to identify a mentor who not only had great general experience, but was also skilled in my interest areas.

> Stay in "rookie mode" and work hard. Learn as much as possible to develop and refine your skills.

I encourage you to become a life-long learner by aggressively seeking knowledge and building expertise.

Who has been your Example?

While in high school, I had a part-time job at the local Kmart. It was there that I first experienced outstanding leadership and learned what I was genuinely passionate about. A new manager, David Tyree, was a gifted and inspirational leader. He enjoyed getting to know me and regularly noticed and appreciated my contributions. It was evident that he accomplished much more than other managers. Even the lazy kids were engaged and getting things done when he worked. It was seemingly simple stuff, but enough to spark my interest in how he led and why people worked so hard for him. That question led to my business management major in college and a particular interest in why people do what they do. I knew then that my career would include inspiring people, and I would work hard to become the best I could be doing it.

An engaged and inspirational leader is a game-changer. Spend some time thinking about the people you have worked with who were particularly passionate about what they did. It felt different, right? Are you passionate about what you do and enjoy doing it? If not, or if you find yourself on a career plateau, I encourage you to engage in it differently. A change in perspective is often enough to "restart your engine" or look for a new opportunity to find your passion.

> When you find your passion, you will find your path, and with focused persistence, you will maximize your potential.

Because we are all unique and bring our own strengths and interests, we can define leadership in our own way. As a leader, the human connection is everything, and how well we can tap into our peoples' strengths and encourage their growth ultimately determines our success. You have a unique opportunity to impact others, don't waste it.

Mentors

As mentioned, I received excellent advice about choosing mentors early in my career. People generally select mentors for various reasons (someone strong in areas you're not, someone who has strengths in your strength area, someone who has overall experience in your field of choice, etc.). Start with at least one mentor who will help you soar with your strengths and has excellent experience overall. That said, once you decide how to approach choosing mentors, aim high. Choose the best person available to you, and if all else is equal, choose the person in the most significant role—the most elevated position. Most people are intimidated to do so, but I've found those folks to be very willing mentors who always set higher expectations for me. Choosing high also puts some healthy pressure on you to value the relationship and put consistent effort into it. For me, choosing high was the president of Target, and late in my career, I was thrilled to have the former CEO as an informal mentor. Solid mentors can be like a rocket engine fueling your path forward. If you're willing to put in the work (the fuel) with the guidance of invested mentors and coaches (the ignition) and apply a strong passion for continuous learning, you'll reach astounding heights.

> Identify mentors early and invest in those relationships.

Mentors can come from all areas of your life and experiences. My leadership journey started when I was very young with sports in grade school. We were fortunate to have a gym teacher and soccer coach who was a recent immigrant from Czechoslovakia and he is an example of a mentor with a significantly different background and life experiences. I learned so much more from him as a result of those differences. He was a skilled coach and soccer player and taught me the importance of refining my game with basic skills, practice, and hard work. All of these values contributed to my success in soccer and life. Interestingly, that coach and mentor stayed with me in a way. In high school, he was the assistant soccer coach, and by the time I was in college, he was the coach at a neighboring university. In his later years, I again ran into him as the gym teacher at my youngest son Kyle's middle school. Thank you, Coach Milan Mader!

Chapter 3
Laughter

Laughter is one of a successful team's most essential ingredients (or symptoms). Is there a more surefire way to bring joy to others? This ingredient directly impacts a team's culture. In my experience, it also encourages people to take risks since it helps build stronger relationships and, as a result, the confidence to offer suggestions or ask for help. As the leader, it's your role to encourage and participate in fun to keep things appropriately light, resulting in wide-open lines of communication. I always encouraged my leadership team to have lunch together as much as possible. As with our daily supper at home when I was a kid, it improved communication, offered opportunities to share stories, and strengthened relationships.

In addition, the medical community tells us that

laughter has many other benefits. Laughter strengthens your immune system, reduces pain, improves mood, reduces stress, eases anxiety, and is a natural antidepressant. When you laugh, that incoming burst of fresh air can lower your blood pressure and promote health overall. Laughter increases happiness and can encourage resilience when handling challenging situations. It also creates a sense of belonging and forms stronger bonds between people. Hmmm . . .

> Have lunch together. Use laughter to enhance an open, fun communication style. Laughter enables stronger connections and idea sharing to learn more about each other. "You never know what you're going to get."

Do you hear and see laughter every day at work? If not, your team's culture isn't as strong as it could be. I loved walking up to my team members laughing and reminding them, "This is a NO FUN environment," after which we would all have a good laugh together. It never gets old. Trust me, it's worth the effort to encourage happiness in your team.

Happiness

There are many ways to encourage joy at work on a day-to-day basis. Often those one-on-one interactions —those moments with the people you lead—have the most significant impact. In one of my favorite TED Talks entitled "Everyday Leadership," Drew Dudley shares about small, lollipop moments that can change people's lives. He adds to the effect of his message by giving the gift of a lollipop to involve other senses.[1] It certainly helped me remember. Like Drew, I believe leadership isn't reserved for extraordinary people. We all possess the capability to lead and make a positive impact. As leaders, we need to find that ability, grow and practice it, and then coax it out of our team, all while having fun doing it.

When I first saw Drew's Ted Talk, I couldn't help but think about the "lollipop moments" that have impacted me so far in my career and life. Take some time now to remember those moments in your life and the difference they made for you, especially as you try to create similar meaningful moments for those you lead.

Meetings and Get-Togethers

Successful leaders find ways to keep the team focused and always search for inspiring examples to share. Think about this: As you plan your meeting agendas, are you including something unexpected or sharing something you recently experienced that you found inspiring? Do you change up your format or freshen it up in some way periodically? Do you encourage people on your team to lead the meeting occasionally or cover portions of the session, allowing them a more significant impact on the team and an opportunity to highlight their abilities? That investment in planning and preparing for those moments is invaluable and worth every minute. Your team will credit you for including those extra touches, and all will benefit from the shared content.

Creating memorable moments in your meetings is truly special (personally and collectively) and goes a long way to forming lasting bonds and inspiring, extraordinary results. The impact these meetings can have on moving your team forward is often visible and measurable. Getting your team on the same page is crucial, and the opportunity to inspire heightened engagement is invaluable. While I have worked for leaders that made all meetings mandatory to force people to attend, I have found more success in encouraging attendance and providing unexpected moments, so people don't want to miss them. Giving them the ability to "choose" to attend when appropriate, at least in my experience, invites more involvement and buy-in. It can also help you better understand their commitment to the team and mission.

Planning and structuring activities are one thing, but there is much to be gained from "spur-of-the-moment" or "off-the-cuff" interactions with your team. As you get to know the folks on your team, build an ongoing dialogue with each person (at all levels), increasing your enjoyment and fulfillment and theirs. When you invest in people and engage with them actively, the resulting stronger connections will help build the sense of belonging that we all seek. The best part of my day was often my daily and even hourly walks to see who I'd encounter. I would challenge myself not to leave the conversation without getting at least a chuckle and thanking them for their efforts.

Earlier in my career, I leveraged an excellent, service-related book, *FISH*, with my team. We were doing fun activities (wearing a silly fish hat, doing a fish dance), focusing on the four critical behaviors in the book: be there, make their day, play, and choose your attitude.[2] To recap those activities, we pulled together a large bulletin board with most of my teams' photos wearing one of the goofy fish hats to remind us of our focus areas. Our CEO visited the store in the following weeks and noted the bulletin board, allowing me to share what we were doing. Simple, silly stuff, but it was huge for my team when we added a picture of him doing the fish dance (wearing one of our silly hats) to the bulletin board. When leaders are vulnerable and willing to participate, which he did, the benefits are memorable. That was twenty-plus years ago, still brings a smile, and is something I will never forget. Thank you, Gregg Steinhafel!

The Department of Your Inner Resources... *Choose your attitude, be there, make their day, play from FISH. Yes, what I did at work became family fun as well. I wonder where those hats are now?*

The Role of Gratitude in Bringing Joy

You've likely heard about the power of gratitude, and I can't emphasize it enough. Being grateful for the people on your team and the unique things they bring is a beautiful thing. Expressing gratitude is a tangible way to strengthen your team's foundation and culture. I'd encourage you to practice an activity like "Three Good Things" daily. Think of three things you are grateful for each morning and write them down. It can be small, simple things like a hug from someone you haven't seen recently, a delicious meal, etc. Every new day builds on the last, and your outlook on everything will change positively and quickly. Twenty-one days make a habit, so why not start today?

Identify three things you are grateful for each day and write them down.

As a leader, expressing your gratitude for others will make a massive difference for your team and enhance your life in many ways. The connection you have with each individual on your team is the most important thing. When you genuinely share those things about a person you're grateful for, even if it's simple, the benefits will be surprising. Remember, each new day is a gift, and it's up to you to honor and do something with it.

Gratitude is a powerful thing, even if it is a day late. While as leaders we strive to be "on" all the time, we inevitably miss the mark sometimes. Revisit those instances in the past few days when you were not the best version of yourself and reflect on how you could have handled things differently. What steps can you take to demonstrate gratitude after missing the initial opportunity?

Chapter 4
Luck

Many believe that people make their good and bad fortune, and that it's actually possible to enhance the "luck" people experience in their lives if they're willing to consider it as a matter of conscious choice. You've likely heard that top golfers like Jack Nichlaus and Tiger woods visualize each shot before they swing—the same idea is accurate with luck. You have to believe it! We are what we think about; if we consider ourselves "lucky," we'll experience more of it.

> *"Sometimes the biggest problem is in your head. You've got to believe you can play a shot instead of wondering where your next bad shot is coming from."*
>
> — Jack Nicklaus

If you don't believe you're lucky but want to change that, a good starting point is to increase your efforts to help and serve others. It's all about perspective, and looking outside of yourself typically yields positive results. There's a famous Zig Ziglar quote: *"You can get whatever you want in life by helping others get what they want."*

People who consider themselves lucky are often very confident and generate good fortune by doing and believing in several things. They're skilled at seeing opportunities and freely sharing them. They make "lucky" decisions without hesitation by trusting their gut and creating self-fulfilling prophecies via a positive approach and strong interpersonal connections. As I think about the people in my life who are exceptionally "lucky," their brighter overall outlook and ability to convey confidence seem to transform bad luck into good regularly. Sometimes it seems like magic.

We all probably know someone like my friend Jon who, as I like to say, "shits gold." He's entertaining and upbeat, invests in relationships freely, and always brings others along. He is a "connector" and goes out of his way to make others feel welcome and involved, which is a true gift. Regardless of the situation or who's involved, he makes all the right moves (seemingly without effort), and every situation or outcome inevitably turns gold. Isn't it true that those who seem the most "lucky" are those with attitudes like Jon's? How many people do you know who consciously try to do three unexpected acts of kindness daily, bringing joy to other peoples' lives? Some may call them lucky, but I tend to believe it goes well beyond that and comes down to one of the topics I'll talk about in the next section: Optimism.

Do three simple acts of kindness each day (or maybe start with one).

Notes and Thoughts:

Section Two
Your Approach Matters

"One person in pursuit of excellence raises the standards of everyone around them. Strive to be your best and inspire others to be their best today."

— Jon Gordon

Chapter 5
Optimism

The second letter, in *L-O-V-E*, leads me to my "O" focus areas: Optimism, Ownership, and Openness. Great leaders tend to be optimistic people, and those leaders believe and convey confidence in each person on the team *and* in the team overall. In many ways, the difference between good and great leaders is often how optimistic they are and how optimism impacts their lives. Many successful people have an upbeat approach to life. Sure, there's a lot of hard work involved in their success, but that underlying positive belief in their abilities makes all the difference.

If you don't consider yourself an optimistic person, there's still hope. We all have the ability to change our perspectives. Focus consistently on small positive steps (three good things, etc.) and build from there. It may be difficult and take persistence and focus, but you can do it.

As a leader, consistently bringing a positive mindset and your best self to the role will ensure success. One thing that helped me was to fill my office with meaningful notes, pieces of recognition, pictures (memories), quotes, etc., all of which I playfully referred to as "shit for my shelf."

One of these was a poem by Charles Swindoll, of which an excerpt is shown below.

> "... *Attitude, to me, is more important than facts. It is more important than the past, than education, money, circumstances, failure, success, and what other people think or say or do. It is more important than appearance, giftedness, or skill. It will make or break a company ... a church ... a home. The remarkable thing is that we choose every day regarding the attitude we will embrace for that day. We cannot change our past ... we cannot change the fact that people will act in a certain way. We cannot change the inevitable. .... I am convinced that life is ten percent what happens to me and ninety percent how I react to it. And so it is with you ... we are in charge of our attitudes."* [1]

I reread that message frequently as I arrived for the day. Think about that for a minute. Ninety

Percent! I'll take those odds for sure. It sounds cheesy, but it's true—your attitude does determine your altitude.

The Pygmalion Effect

When you set high expectations for your team and communicate belief and confidence in them, it will lead to higher performance—often significantly higher. That phenomenon is known as the Pygmalion Effect and has been proven in several studies throughout history. In one study, Robert Rosenthal and Lenore Jacobson examined the influence of teachers' expectations on students' performance. The teachers were informed that twenty percent of the students were extremely intelligent, but the "gifted" children were actually chosen at random. All students were tested initially and then retested at the end of the study. While both groups showed improvements, those described as especially intelligent experienced much more significant gains in their IQ points. The researchers attributed that result to the Pygmalion Effect. Teachers paid more attention to gifted students, offering more support and encouragement than otherwise.[2]

Like teachers, leaders can significantly impact their teams' performance and growth by expressing confidence in them and setting high expectations.

When I think back to people I've worked with where The Pygmalion Effect was especially evident, a young woman immediately comes to mind. She was in beauty school and working part-time in the cosmetics area of the flagship store when I first met her. It was immediately clear to me she had something special, although I'm not sure she realized it. Despite dealing with some challenges in her personal life, with encouragement, she took on several challenging roles, including moving into her first executive supervisory position. She eventually became one of the strongest executives on my team and recently graduated from college. She's now leading her first Target store team. Stephanie, you're exceptional, and your team is lucky to have you as their leader. I look forward to continuing to watch you soar in whatever you choose to do.

Anyone can do whatever they put their mind to, especially if they have leaders who show true confidence in them. If you encourage them and provide them the opportunity to engage in things that they are passionate about, soaring with their strengths, the outcome will likely be outstanding.

"Technology is nothing. What's important is that you have faith in people, that they are basically good and smart, and if you give them the tools and encouragement, they will do wonderful things with them."

— Steve Jobs

Well-Being as It Relates to Optimism:

Generally, optimistic people are more likely to maintain better physical health and are less at risk for disease. Exercise, especially done first-thing in the morning, engages your brain differently and positively sets up your day. Studies have shown that as little as twenty to thirty minutes per day can make a significant difference, regardless of when you do it.

Emotional well-being is also essential—we're often our worst enemies in that area. We frequently think negatively and doubt ourselves (self-sabotage), which takes its toll over time. Auto-suggestions or affirmations can counter those thoughts. Tony Robbins offers, as an example, "All I need is within me now." Years ago, I benefited from using that affirmation for the first time, giving me extra confidence before an important interview. It's proven helpful numerous times for me and others I shared it with.

Whenever I face a challenge or difficult situation, I do that same self-talk to this day.

If you repeat a positive affirmation of your choosing fifteen to twenty times in the morning and evening for several weeks, you'll feel the difference. Even if you don't initially believe it, the resulting change in mindset can significantly impact your career and life. Creating a daily routine around positive self-talk that works for you may surprise you. Why not try it? The Law of Attraction essentially states that positive or negative thoughts bring positive or negative experiences in a person's life. If you believe in the Law of Attraction, as I do, you may want to try focusing on the positive.

Physical and Mental Well-Being

I have an entirely new level of optimism and energy after starting a daily walking routine. It's often a highlight of my day. In addition to physical activity and resulting health benefits, it allows for some time alone with my thoughts, which can be rejuvenating. If you don't have time for a walk or exercise, I encourage you to identify some affirmations or short reads to help you start your day with a positive mindset. Later, as you wrap up your day and start winding down before bed, spending some time thinking about the best parts and being grateful can make a huge difference.

Failing Equals Winning

We all make mistakes and fail at times. It's part of the process and, in my view, a positive part. Failing helps build the character you need to succeed as you navigate even more challenging situations. How you respond to those instances makes all the difference. Think positive! When you experience difficulty and make mistakes, it provides opportunities to spring forward to new learning and possibilities. You may have heard the idea of "failing up or failing forward." If you view failures as learning moments, you'll be much further ahead. History tells us that the most successful people fail more often than others, and those failures ignite the passion for the next triumph. Did you know that Thomas Edison tried and failed ten thousand times before perfecting the light bulb? We all encounter adversity (even negative self-talk) regularly. Often, most of us don't respond in the best ways after failures or mistakes. However, making a small positive change in mindset when you fail or make a mistake can change your life. Just imagine how significant the impact can be on the people you lead when you guide them through the same "outlook adjustment."

One of my "failing forward" moments was when

I put together a roadmap to encourage Target to spend the money to remodel the flagship store. As a result of our significant guest traffic and everyday wear-and-tear, maintaining our brand was getting more challenging. Since our store's business and retail were changing dramatically (things like order pick-up, expanded food options, larger Starbucks, and larger public restrooms), we needed to keep up to stay competitive. The roadmap was a reasonably comprehensive document, including a detailed sales analysis, drawings of necessary changes, and how the change would significantly improve sales and profit. It also outlined the changes to the team environment (ie. improved team member service center including larger employee lockers, expanded and updated lounge area, and a more private conference room) to positively impact our team culture. With the help of several on my team, we prepared display boards with the key components that I used to make my presentation. Despite my passion and excitement around this project, it didn't go according to my plan. I owned my failure because I didn't thoroughly sell the project and didn't learn enough about the formula used by upper management to make that type of decision. I learned, stayed positive, and continued building our business. I leveraged my relationships with "HQ friends" to try new ideas in the store, laying the groundwork for what I knew was necessary to ensure our long-term success. Sometime later, as we started updating the store, I realized that every component I had included in my roadmap was indeed part of the remodeling plan, plus some.

If you feel strongly about something, even if you stumble initially, stay confident, be persistent, and stick with it.

Chapter 6
Ownership

As the leader, everything that happens within your team—every struggle and failure—is your responsibility, and you must understand and embrace that. If someone on your team is failing, look in the mirror first. What is your role in that failure, and what can you do now?

Ownership is all-inclusive and involves assigning responsibility for what happens and when, and communicating to ensure everyone is in the loop on the plan. It consists of answering questions whenever there's uncertainty, empowering lower-level leaders to have a high level of ownership, and encouraging them to do the same with their teams.

I firmly believe there are no bad teams, just bad leaders. Reflecting on my career, I can recall a couple of situations where groups I was a part of (our bigger team) struggled endlessly despite our best efforts. Those failures were rooted in issues or gaps in ownership with our leader and that person's leader. The boss constantly applied pressure by micro-managing, being too controlling, and insisting that we push more on our teams. Inevitably, when leadership (at the top) changed for whatever reason in both situations, our team and our results changed dramatically, and we began to flourish in many ways.

I recall the CEO and the president of grocery walking the store and evaluating our food areas, thinking that any issues we had must be present in all neighboring stores. On that particular day, we were in rough shape. Due to some recent leadership changes (along with schedule and process issues), we struggled more than we had in a long time. I came upon them as they were wrapping up and saw that they noticed our issues.

After I greeted them and acknowledged what they saw, I told them the issues were my own and not symptomatic of any more significant, widespread problems in the area. On an unrelated visit shortly after, that same day, I walked the store with our regional senior vice-president, so I had to own my failure with him as well.

You've likely heard the statement, "Trust but verify." In this case, I failed as a leader when I failed to "verify." As I dug in deeper following the visits, I learned that communication within our team had broken down and that some key team members on the front line doing the work didn't feel like their input was needed or valued. I wasn't close enough to the leader of the team and his processes and it cost us.

Stuff happens sometimes. Acknowledge it, own it, and move to correct it. That was a vulnerable moment for me, and I learned from it.

Chapter 7
Openness
Appreciating Differences

The flagship store was unlike any other and would provide many challenges that tested everything I had learned. It was the first truly urban store, and Target had much to learn. We wanted to be sure that our team represented the community. It was challenging. Our business peaked during the week and was largely business professionals that worked downtown. In the evenings and on weekends, the local community was our guests. My leadership team initially, while appropriately diverse and representative of the community we served, came from stores in the surrounding area where their store's business was mostly Saturday and Sunday. In addition, we hired four hundred-plus hourly team members who came from all walks of life and circumstances. The best part of their day was often coming to work. We all had so much to learn. The initial team was highly diverse. Early on, we put a world map on the wall in our team area and asked everyone to put a small flag on the map indicating where "home" was. Incredibly, we had 42 countries represented, and English was the second language for many of them. Though a gift, this diversity presented many challenges, as training was much more hands-on, the videos weren't adequate, and the wide variety of customs was unfamiliar to many of us. We used interpreters, other outside services, and bilingual people on the team to help bridge those gaps. Over the years, it was clear that our team was much more robust due to its differences and diversity, and we made every effort possible to value each person and the things that made them unique. Though full of people from many different backgrounds, unity and togetherness persisted in our teams.

The store was set to open on October 15, 2001, and we were well into the pre-opening process when time stopped. The Twin Towers and the Pentagon were in flames. It's hard to find words to describe the moment accurately, but I remember it like it was yesterday. We gathered closely in a circle and shared a few minutes of silent prayer. For those few moments, we were one, supporting each other. Within hours we heard that the brother of one of my leaders was likely in one of the buildings and soon afterward learned that several other team members had received terrible news. We immediately heard concerns from outside our walls that local high-rise buildings in the city could also be potential targets, and although every team member received the option of going home for the day, I don't remember anyone leaving.

We were in New York City recently and visited the 911 Memorial. What a powerful and emotionally moving experience! My thoughts went immediately to that store and my team. Just as with the people of New York and our Country, that event brought my team together in a way that made us stronger for what was ahead.

Starting with the pre-opening process, we proved that people of all cultures, styles, ages, and levels of experience could work together, live together, and thrive together.

My teams were always multi-generational, so there was a constant self-imposed challenge to keep things fresh and ensure that I connected with my entire team regardless of age, background, or style. If you start with building a solid foundational relationship, are open to new perspectives, *and* can appreciate each other's differences, you can lead them all. It makes leading fresh and invigorating. Have fun with it.

Being open to new ideas and different ways of

doing things is essential as we recognize, appreciate, and truly value the diversity of our team. As leaders, we need to identify each person's strengths and do our best to put them in situations that allow them and, as a result, the team to soar.

Getting to know and understand your team well, including where they are in their development, is essential, and there are many ways to do that.

HBD Instrument

William Edward "Ned" Herrmann was a creativity researcher known for his whole-brain methods and is considered the "Father of Brain Dominance Technology." He was a pioneer in expanding the understanding of the brain in a close-up view as a four-quadrant system regarding thinking styles. I have successfully identified strengths by using what is known as the "Herrmann Brain Dominance (HBD) Instrument." His instrument essentially assesses each person's preferences and strengths in four quadrants and graphs it in a way that shows your thinking style visually.[1]

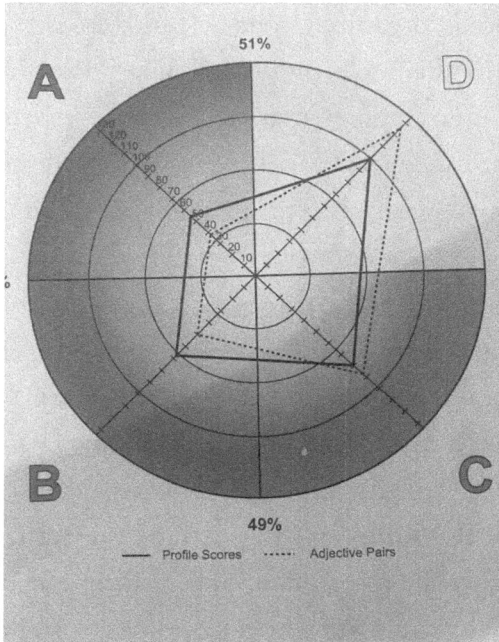

This is my graph. As you can see, my strongest
quadrant is D (Yellow), followed by C (Red).
In addition to knowing your own,
understanding which quadrants your team
falls into (what their thinking styles are) will
be very helpful in leading them to success.

The **A (Blue) quadrant** (top left) is logical, fact-based, analytical thinking. People strong in this thinking style prefer collecting and analyzing data, understanding how things work, judging ideas based on facts, and critical/logical thinking. Since this quadrant is my lowest area, I always looked for those skills and tendencies in others as I put my teams together.

The **B (Green) quadrant** (bottom left) is

structured, organized, and clear thinking. People strong in this style prefer following directions and step-by-step implementation. As you can see, this is also not a strength area for me which presented an excellent opportunity to highlight those qualities in others.

The **C (Red) quadrant** (lower right) is interpersonal thinking using emotions and senses to connect. People with this thinking style prefer listening to and expressing ideas, looking for personal meaning, sensory input, and group interaction. I refer to this group as "huggers" as they're strong in interpersonal connection and utilize emotions to influence things. As you can see by my graph, I'm a hugger.

The **D (Yellow) quadrant** (top right) is for creative, innovative, and fresh thinking. This area is my dominant quadrant, and these strengths drove my success in all areas of my life. People strong in this thinking style prefer looking at the big picture. They're self-starters, like to challenge assumptions, and tend toward long-term thinking. They're also visual learners and tend to be risk-takers.

Several of my teams have benefited by taking the HBD Instrument over the years. It's been helpful in how I lead overall and how I set the individuals on my team up for success. If you understand the concept well, I don't believe you have to complete the instrument to benefit from its message.

Any tension or disagreements between people tend to come from differences. This can be differences in experience, background, preferences, and thinking styles. Folks must work through some of those differences by finding value in what makes each person unique. Recognizing the thinking style differences early and sharing them has been an enormous asset in leading my teams and driving results. Once individuals who didn't initially connect well understood more about their style preferences, the entire team benefited. Obviously, it's far better to appreciate differences between individuals than to disagree with one another. Once you become familiar with the four quadrants and the benefits that people strong in each one bring, then you're more prepared to set them up for success. It guided me in many ways, including how I assigned projects and resolved interpersonal struggles, among others things.

When we built the team to open the flagship store, we chose people with various backgrounds and experience levels. In addition, and more importantly, we made conscious decisions regarding their thinking styles, which served us well. Generally speaking, when you don't connect well with someone, your tendency should be to go towards that person rather than away from them, as they likely have something you don't and vice versa.

Years ago, a former boss shared with me that he tried to surround himself with people who were brighter than himself and had different perspectives. Having all views represented when making decisions ensured the best possible result. Since I was involved in those discussions, I saw it work regularly. He practiced the "work your strengths and hire your weaknesses" philosophy, and I have followed that lead throughout my career. It, too, has served me well.

I'm a D/C (Yellow/Red) quadrant thinker, meaning I operate in the D (Yellow) quadrant area most frequently followed by the C (Red) quadrant. In other words, I'm right-brained. I look at challenges and problem-solving differently, especially when people (like my team) are involved. I'm a self-starter, always seeking new ways to approach things and inspire others. Due to the investment in building relationships early on, I knew my team well. Experience with the HBDI allowed me to leverage their strengths and tendencies more frequently, which moved the team forward quickly. People encouraged to work on projects that complement their thinking style tend to be happier, resulting in stronger engagement and better results.

Practical experience with HBDI opened my eyes to the value of having all perspectives represented on my team. Consider different thinking styles, backgrounds, and experiences when you have open positions on your team.

Interestingly, I married a D/C (Yellow/Red) quadrant thinker, and she, too, happens to be a Virgo. Yikes! People say that "opposites attract," and, well, let me just say that I understand why. Ha! In reality, it's fantastic most of the time. We feed off each other and enjoy being creative and sharing perspectives. We can solve virtually any problem . . . eventually.

Notes and Thoughts:

Section Three

The More You Risk, the Greater the Potential Reward

"Only those who dare to fail greatly can ever achieve greatly."

— Robert F. Kennedy

Chapter 8
Vulnerability

The third letter in L-O-**V**-E is where I want to highlight three "V" ingredients: being Vulnerable, having a Vision, and Volition. We all have opportunities to share our stories, and when it comes to leading, you must acknowledge and share yours. I especially encourage you to share your "failure stories" in detail and not leave out the pain and embarrassment you felt. When you're vulnerable and authentic, it will resonate well, and your team will feel more connected to you.

Since many leaders often view their team's mistakes as failures and weaknesses, many tend to hold those experiences tight to the vest. However, when leaders share their failures (and related learning), it encourages their team to do the same. Admit when you're wrong, take ownership, and move on.

Be Courageous

Who you are is non-negotiable. Be confident and never compromise your beliefs. Being vulnerable is contagious, and it's essential to remember that we need trust to be vulnerable, and we need to be vulnerable to have trust. Even if it's uncomfortable, show up, tell your story, and be authentic. When you model the way as a leader, your team will be more connected to you and more willing to be vulnerable as they lead their teams.

Vulnerability in leadership wasn't always natural for me. I learned through many different experiences that it benefitted my team to know me holistically. However, one specific night changed my life and the way I lead in vulnerability forever.

It was late one evening, just before the store closed, and I was in my first store team leadership role. It had been a typical day, and the initial closing announcement had just reminded our guests that we would close soon. I was in my office, which over-looked the front of the store and checkout area. Suddenly, I heard a loud noise and screaming. I turned to look through the window and saw people frantically running and scattering in all directions. Within a few seconds, I was at the front doors, trying to figure out what was happening. I saw the terror on the faces of numerous guests and people on my team, including my security person, who was holding his bloodied arm. He could barely get words out, but I understood enough to learn that he had stopped a shoplifter who pulled out a gun and shot him. After quickly ensuring that people inside were ok and that I had leaders in place to talk with them, I went outside to the parking lot. People pointed toward a car nearby, where I could see someone lying on the asphalt. As I approached, I could see it was my cart attendant Gary. His eyes were glazed over, and I couldn't tell if he was breathing. Immediately someone ran up and said, "The guy shot him! He shot him!" We both looked at Gary, and without speaking, we tore his button-down shirt open. I noticed what looked like a small entry wound in his chest just to the right of the center as I leaned closer to see if he was breathing. At that moment, I was tapped on the shoulder by a police officer, and as I turned, I saw an ambulance pulling into the lot. It all happened so fast.

Within minutes the store was a crime scene, and everyone had to be interviewed by the police before leaving, which wasn't completed until well after three in the morning. In the following hours, my inner voice screamed as I tried to process what had happened. So many thoughts were running through my head, and so much uncertainty. Why couldn't it have been me and not Gary? How do I ensure my team is informed and, more importantly, that they're all ok? After several hours of waiting for the Police to release the building, including significant time alone with my thoughts, I remember telling myself, "Murray, you can handle this, you're at your best in challenging situations, and you can lead your team through this." I didn't realize it then but have since learned that talking to myself as I did gave me the additional confidence I needed. My "distanced self-talk," which I came to appreciate and understand much later in my career, allowed me to mentally take a step back from the situation to do the right things in supporting my team.

> Positive self-talk, even amidst personal insecurities and extreme stress can make all the difference.

We lost Gary that night, which was devastating for all involved—his family, the community, and our team. He was a friend to many, myself included. Gary's wife, Carol, and one of their kids also worked on my team, which was a blessing as I could ensure she had access to counseling or anything else she needed.

I didn't sleep that night and was back in the building by seven that morning. One of the first people I saw after arriving was Kevin Norris. He was the head of assets protection for our area and had driven nearly three hours down from Minneapolis to help. His first words were, "How are you doing?" After a few minutes of updating him, he told me what he had already put in motion, which included getting counselors and support help as well as connecting me with HQ media relations. Hence, I knew how to handle the press, who already wanted to talk with me. He then took on helping me update some of the critical partners, etc. He was terrific, and his support, encouragement, and friendship in those moments were beyond amazing and unforgettable.

I don't remember the words I chose that day following the shooting, but I remember the names and faces of many who shared the experience. I also remember many conversations and tears from the following days. As a result of that horrendous event and those moments we shared, we became much closer. The memory of how my team members embraced and helped each other left a permanent impression on me. I can still recall the anxiety and worry I felt as I didn't know how to handle this situation, especially with meeting the needs of my team. I struggled to express how I felt and, thankfully, got support from the professionals on the scene in the days and weeks following. It was apparent that I needed to do more to get to know each person on my team and that I still had much to learn about vulnerability and opening up.

That night and the days that followed changed my life forever. I had always considered myself a people person, but now everything was different. This tragedy taught me the importance of vulnerability, listening closely to people's words, and trying harder to feel what they feel. It was ok to be vulnerable and, in this case, emotional. It also reinforced the lessons I had learned from my parents growing up—I learned the importance of trusting others. Those moments helped shape the leader I became. I realized I didn't always have to be the "strong" leader and the person who had all of the answers.

Risk and Vulnerability

When I visited a friend in Hawaii a few years back, he shared a story about a family member that inspired me. Kori, who has special needs and generally doesn't like anything touching her face, was very excited about a trip to the "secret beach" where she would see some fish and, more importantly, sea turtles. She loves sea turtles. She was so excited that she wore her goggles the entire ride to the beach despite her anxiety about having things touch her face. Her courage and positive energy inspired my thinking about risk-taking and pushing yourself to be the best you can be: "Like a turtle, you can only move forward if you stick your neck out."

I like to search for inspiration while on vacation via reading (usually several books), and it has become a running joke with my family as they wonder if I'll ever join them at the swim-up bar. This time, however, my inspiration came from Kori's story.

As I started my first leadership meeting when I returned, I wore goggles and a snorkel to kick things off and shared Kori's story. We needed to improve and drive positive progress as a team. It was a perfect fit. We were energetic and upbeat about our challenges and how to assess them. We laughed throughout the discussion, probably because I kept the goggles on (which fogged up several times).

Always move forward. Thanks to Kori's inspiration: "Like a turtle, you can only move forward if you stick your neck out." Step outside your comfort zone and try something new—"Risk It!"

As I wrapped up the meeting, I gave each team member a miniature bobblehead turtle for their desks that I brought back from our trip. I wanted to inspire them to stick their neck out to help move our team forward if necessary.

I received great feedback from the team following that meeting, and the almost immediate positive energy and progress around the topics discussed told me that it resonated with them.

When I look at risk-taking and vulnerability, I think more about it from an individual perspective. Generally speaking, as long as the risk will move the team forward and no one gets hurt, it's likely worth taking. Take risks by stepping outside comfort zones and trying something new.

Failing = Growth = Success

Mistakes will happen if you and your team are aggressive and pushing forward to make real progress. I like to refer to those errors or mistakes as "Oh Shit Moments" and something to celebrate as long as the person making it acknowledges the mistake and learns from it. The goal would be not to repeat the same error. As a leader, I believe it's essential to talk about those situations and thank the team members for taking the risk and resolving it.

I remember hearing about Chip Brewer's leadership story as CEO at Callaway Golf. He told his team in their journey to reinvent their company, "I do not care how we have to do it and how many things we have to fail on; we aren't going to launch products that aren't demonstratively superior and pleasingly different."[1] Chip Brewer believed that failure is not final, instead, it's feedback.

"Failure is not fatal, but failure to change might be."

— John Wooden

Stand Tall and Show Your Value

It's important to note that not all leaders (or bosses) look at failure this way, and sometimes they may respond negatively and even punitively. Over the years, I've counseled countless leaders who have experienced pain from their supervisor due to their poor decisions or actions, and it can be genuinely devastating at the time. Depending on their experience with those demanding situations, it can even derail the careers of less experienced folks.

Many years ago, my wife dealt with a stressful situation at work and shared her story with a trusted vendor partner. He made eye contact with her and offered some of the best advice I had ever heard. He told her to ***Stand tall and show your value.*** When you're dealing with a challenging situation, or someone on your team is, there's simply no better advice to share.

On April 23, 1910, about a year after leaving office, Theodore Roosevelt gave a famous speech, "Citizenship in a Republic," often referred to as "The Man in The Arena" speech. It's one of his most quoted speeches, and what follows is a part of that speech that I wanted to share.

> *"It's not the critic that counts; not the man who points out how the strong man stumbles or where the doer of deeds could have done them better. The credit belongs to the man who is actually in the arena, whose face is marred by dust and sweat and blood; who strives valiantly; who errs, who comes short again and again, because there is no effort without error and shortcoming; but who does actually strive to do the deeds; who knows great enthusiasms, the great devotions; who spends himself in a worthy cause; who at best knows, in the end, the triumph of high achievement, and who at the worst, if he fails, at least fails while daring greatly."*[2]

— Theodore Roosevelt

When you make a mistake, acknowledge it and move quickly to correct it. Stand tall and show your value!

Chapter 9
Vision

Numerous books and articles focus on the importance of a vision, and I encourage you to do some homework. Learn and gain understanding so you have clarity on developing your own vision. Your vision is the difference between how things are today and where you feel they can or will be in the future. It includes those areas and activities you're passionate about and establishes the framework to build and clarify your purpose and goals. Your goals are the steps you take toward realizing your vision and should be updated often. In my experience, having some visual representation of your vision is often helpful, whether it's written down (process charts, people plans, etc.) or through pictures.

Vision Boards

Since I'm a right-brained thinker, I've often struggled to develop action plans and step-by-step implementation strategies. Having left-brain thinkers on my team and including them in that process was necessary—they ensured we didn't miss a beat. I often used a "Vision Board," a visual reminder of our goals, to keep things progressing at work and home.

Have you ever had a project on your to-do list that always seemed to get pushed down the list? We had a small raised eight by eight deck for years, and I could imagine what I wanted to do about enlarging it. Nothing happened, and literal years went by. After I went through numerous deck-building magazines and realized what I wanted for a new deck, things started to happen. I believe the extra visual step of cutting out pictures and adding them to my vision board was the catalyst to getting the project done in time for our youngest son's graduation. One of my big regrets was that I didn't make the vision board earlier because we didn't have much time to enjoy it after downsizing a few years later. The key here is to ensure your goal remains top of mind, and enlisting other senses by creating visual inspiration helps.

The same is true for children. I have friends that create vision boards with their kids every year to help them focus on what they want to achieve during the year (sports, activities, reading, etc.), which is super cool and something I wish I had known about earlier. What a great example to set our kids up to win in life, as they'll surely accomplish more each year because you helped them through that exercise!

Like parents, as a leader you must have an exciting, challenging, and ever-present vision for your team. Do what is necessary to keep goals in mind for yourself and your team and build your routines around it. Talk about them and share them frequently with others. Measure successes against them, recognize people for contributions toward them, etc. Remember, if you want your team to invest in your vision and goals, you must first invest in them as people and leaders. That investment starts when you establish your foundational relationship and learn more about them. It grows as you continue to work together and better understand where they are in their development. That investment in them creates an opportunity to co-create the path together, including the steps involved (goals), which ensures success.

When William "Dabo" Swinney was Clemson's assistant coach, the head coach resigned and he was named the interim for the remaining games of the season. The Board of Trustees committed to providing him with an opportunity to interview to be the new head coach if things went well. They told him they wanted the football program to be like some of the other great programs in the country, and Dabo replied by saying that he appreciated their vision but saw something much bigger. His vision was to create a program where others wanted to be like Clemson. His passion for the program's future was evident, and after a strong showing the rest of that year, he won the job.

Immediately after he got the job, he met with the players alone—with no other coaches present—and shared his vision. He asked them to be all-in and join him in dreaming big, believing in their abilities and what was ahead for them as a team. Dabo's vision became a reality due to his firm, focused belief in his players, his clear and specific goals, and his ability to inspire his team to support that vision. Clemson has had significant success since Dabo took over as coach. They won two National Championships in three years within just a few years, and his teams now regularly compete for the Championship.

Subsequent years have been challenging for Clemson as they graduated numerous highly talented players to the NFL. Despite losing more games recently, Dabo hasn't changed. He remains optimistic, hopeful, encouraging, and energetic. He shared that he's been able to teach his team lessons he wouldn't be able to otherwise, which will equip and strengthen them for their future—a great example of how a positive leader handles adversity and disappointment. I especially love this encouragement for his players: "Always let the light that shines inside of you be brighter than the light shining on you." Such a great leader!

The Importance of a Plan and Goals

All that we've discussed up to this point is worthless without a vision, including a roadmap with a clear direction in the form of focused plans and goals. Once you have your goals, it becomes about building routines and habits to move you toward them. Small consistent improvements each day are key.

Historically, learning every piece of the business (your career of choice) step-by-step was viewed as the best way to move forward and succeed. While hard work will always be an essential ingredient for success, a focused plan and clear goals that impact you and benefit others can significantly enhance the trajectory of your advancement. Write them down and refer to your plan frequently. A few years ago, the popular advice was to create a short-term five-year plan and build from that for your longer-range career plan. Tighter timeframes within your planning are more appropriate these days. Those entering the workforce want and demand more frequent touchpoints. They want to feel appreciated, valued, and included—and working with tighter goals and plans supports that.

Before opening the flagship store, I was standing in the skyway outside our soon-to-open store with our company's CEO. At that time, Bob Ulrich was also leading Marshall Fields and Mervyns California, the two sibling companies to Target. I had done my homework and was ready to make my case. I wanted to adjust the opening time for the in-store Starbucks to capture the business of the downtown workers heading to the office. I knew that typically Starbucks' busiest time of day was during the two hours before we planned to open. I made my pitch after updating him on our grand opening celebration plan. He listened intently, paused politely, and said, "Murray, I'm only interested in selling coffee if it's part of the shopping experience." It was instantaneous—a "no" with clarity. He was brilliant and highly focused, and he's someone who defined Target and established the foundation from which more recent leaders built new roadmaps. He had a plan and executed it well. I'm so grateful and fortunate to have felt his impact on my career.

When you establish your dreams and goals, the critical thing to remember is to aim high and develop clear timeframes to re-evaluate and adjust. Stay focused on your path and plan, and do the work.

Chapter 10
Volition

Have you met someone who could will things to happen without help or support from anyone else? That "will-power" or capability to decide on and commit to a specific course of action is known as Volition. One of my earliest memories was of my parents instilling in me that if I worked hard, I could do whatever I wanted to do and be whatever I wanted to be. That was my first lesson on volition.

Volition is the most powerful force in human behavior. It's the power of choice. Every day you can make a positive choice or a negative choice. You choose your attitude for that day. You can choose to work hard, stand out, trust in others by following your heart, and pursue your dreams. It's about the decision to pursue something with every ounce of your energy and focus.

Some confuse volition with motivation; while they are related, there is a difference. Motivation is the desire to do something, whereas volition goes beyond that and is the commitment to achieve something amazing.

As I reflect on my life, there are numerous times when my volition fueled my teams forward. There are examples all around us in sports and life of the same.

After a recent match at the Wimbledon Tennis Championships, when interviewed after upsetting a ranked player, a young Brit said that since he was five years old, he knew that he'd get to center court at Wimbledon and win. He made a choice when he was very young and committed to doing what was necessary to reach that goal—and many years later, he did it.

Jim Carey is another example. When he was in his early teens, his dad lost his job, and his family hit tough times, including living in a VW van in a relative's yard. At age fifteen, he bombed his first comedy routine on stage, but he kept at it. A year later, he quit school and moved to LA to focus on comedy full-time, and at night would routinely park on Mulholland Drive and visualize his future success. One of those nights, he wrote himself a check for ten million dollars for "acting services rendered," which he dated for Thanksgiving 1995, several years later.

Just before that date, he hit his payday for the movie *Dumb and Dumber*. He put that deteriorated check, which he had kept in his wallet the entire time, in his father's casket.

One more example is Tom Brady—whose volition goes without saying. We all know what he did after being selected 199th in the 2000 draft . . .

You are the CEO of your life—you are the boss of you. You have the power to choose, and with desire and determination–acting on your own volition–great things will happen.

Notes and Thoughts:

Section Four
Enjoy the Hunt!

"A mind that is stretched by a new experience can never go back to its old dimensions."

— Oliver Wendell Holmes

Chapter 11
Energize

My idea is the best idea until I have heard someone else's.
I don't just encourage you to share your perspective; I insist on it.

Those two statements were part of every conversation I had the first time I sat down with leaders joining my team. I wanted them to know their experiences were unique, and I didn't want them to hesitate to share them even if they were new to the team or recently moved into a leadership role for the first time.

Individual Versus Team Mindset

Less experienced leaders were usually very focused on themselves and learning their roles, and without some teaching, they often tended toward having an individual mindset. Similarly, experienced leaders joining the team were often more focused on themselves and their areas than team goals when looking to stand out. Successful leaders encourage their team to be a part of "something bigger," which is the overall team's success. Helping and encouraging each other and having a dedicated team mindset are vital to team cohesiveness and a great culture.

Modeling the way as the leader is important, and when leaders joined my team I made sure to instill that in them. My perspective was that our team is as strong as the combined strengths of everyone on it. Their varied experiences, education, and background, including interpersonal skills, were the reasons we wanted them on the team in the first place.

Keeping it Fresh

It's your responsibility as the leader to keep things fresh and exciting. A vital component is continuously reminding your team, in exciting, inspiring, and creative ways, that they're part of something bigger than themselves—the overall team's success.

Thinking outside of the box is something I value, so I'm always looking for new things. One of the methods I came up with was what I called "TED Tuesdays." Periodically, I would pick one of my favorite Ted Talks (on all subjects, not just business or leadership), show them in our conference room over lunch, and encourage folks to enjoy them while eating. We would show the same talk several times on those Tuesdays, so the entire leadership team and anyone interested would get a chance to view them. The brief conversations about the different talks were enjoyable and often involved things we wouldn't have usually discussed.

Another powerful way to engage your team is to involve them in goal setting (short and long-term goals they care about achieving). As Coach Dabo Swinney did, you'll find that if they're part of the process, the momentum is powerful initially, allowing for visible progress you can build from in short order.

Team Updates and Get-Togethers

Getting the larger group together at least twice a year to clarify goals or make any updates was helpful. Sometimes, it was necessary to get together more frequently when the team struggled or major staff changes occurred. Putting extra effort into planning those meetings using videos, current events, and personal stories made a huge difference. Each included meaningful recognition and a business update to ensure the team was in the loop on our progress. Plus, I always tried to have something unexpected—whether it was being vulnerable (by showing up as Uncle Sam, the Green Man, Yoda, Bob Barker, etc.), by inviting a special guest, or doing some special recognition.

The Power of Storytelling

As you think about your career, you may remember a leader or two who was incredibly inspiring. In my case, there were several people. One, in particular, was exceptional—Bob O'Rourke was a higher-level leader I didn't work with directly (my boss' boss), and he was gifted in inspiring others, especially when storytelling. I learned so much from him and others like him about inspirational leadership.

There were many examples, but one sticks out for me. On this occasion, the group leadership team, including all store team leaders, district team leaders, and regional staff (about eighty people), were together for several days at a resort in northern Minnesota—in "God's Country." That's how the

Boomers in Minnesota refer to it, according to a much younger friend. We had several days of meetings, camaraderie, recognition, and learning.

On the last morning of the meetings, he wrapped up the week after a full day of fun on the lake. He began with a recap, followed by a personal story about his kids that emphasized a component we focused on as a large team the last few days. I don't remember exactly how he got there, but he mentioned he has a personal rule to never walk by a live performer without stopping to watch and listen for at least a few minutes. He shared a story about walking up on a guitar-playing singer at the Mall of America. He painted a picture of the situation that was so clear it felt like we were there with him. I remember him talking about the messages in his songs etc., specifically the two that struck a chord (no pun intended) with him. He recited the words of the song line by line, shared what each one meant to him, and connected the message back to what's most important (family) and enjoying the journey (life). The singer's name is Dan Schwartz, and the song that connected well with me is "Joyride."

Overall, his wrap-up message and delivery were incredible. Here we are, some twenty-plus years later, and it's still crystal clear to me. As he was about to send us back to our homes, he again mentioned the significant impact that the singer and his music had on him. At that point, he pulled a curtain behind him, and there was Dan Schwartz with his guitar. His final song was "Joyride." That moment was a clear tipping point in my leadership journey because it impacted me in the same way I want to impact others—it connected with me emotionally. It was clear he invested time preparing for his presentation which I embraced going forward as I prepared crucial presentations in the future.

Thank you, Bob O'Rourke! I have encountered inspiring leaders during my career and listened to some great speakers, but this particular story hit the mark. I became a better, more inspiring leader that day because you took the extra time to prepare for that moment and because of your gift of storytelling.

Clarifying Your Message: Using Acronyms

Like I chose to use L-O-V-E as an acronym for successful leadership, I would periodically find other words or phrases to keep the team engaged and inspired on our path. This tool gave me more opportunities to inspire the team and drive results. It was my not-so-subtle way of re-stating goals and clarifying our focus while staying on the same path. Some acronyms or focus words that I have used as an example are:

D-A S-Q-U-A-D: During this period, I had a relatively new mix of leaders. My goal was to inspire them to take risks in leading and focus on developing their leadership style D: Dare to lead differently, A: Accelerate you. The challenge was to think like a leader and build strong habits around that, as I knew that would move our team forward faster. Too often, my leadership team got distracted by small details instead of focusing on how to help their team improve or look at things differently. Leaders must understand the specifics, but they can't be so close to the details and process that they lose sight of the overall mission. Simply put, you can't do your job well if you also do someone else's.

> You can't do your job well if you also do someone else's.

Like the fish hats and Drew Dudley and his lollipop, I found it beneficial to include some activities or additional components to engage the team differently. You may remember the scene in Tony Scott's *Top Gun* where Maverick and Goose wrap up a beach volleyball game with their "high-five" handshake while reciting "the need for speed." That was a fun way for them to celebrate after winning the game. At the end of the meeting at which I introduced DA SQUAD, with my entire leadership team involved (twenty five-plus leaders), I presented that same motion in a handshake, but this time with "lead more, do less." It was fun—I insisted each leader on my team greet everyone in the room with our new handshake before they could leave the meeting.

Again, silly, simple stuff, but I still saw leaders having fun with it weeks later, and the energy around DA SQUAD leaped ahead.

Dare	Dare to Lead Differently. Get out of your comfort zone. Take risks to move your team & business forward.
Accelerate	Accelerate You. Set personal development stretch goals and define progress/winning.
Serve	Servant Leadership: To lead is to serve. Provide resources, time, guidance, inspiration for your team. Engage their hearts & minds to work for the team's success.
Quintessential	Quintessential Connections: Understand and leverage our "Dimensions of Difference" to build lasting relationships. Develop expert business owners.
Unwavering	Unwavering Focus on team goals & results. Know your business. Inspect what you expect consistently. Have a plan, own the details & track your results.
Audacious	Audacity: Who you are is non-negotiable. Advocate for yourself, be authentic and never compromise your beliefs. Strive to make others better. Have fun!
Deliberate	Deliberate Practice: Cast your leadership shadow deliberately. Be urgent. Be your best self everyday.

V-A-L-U-E-S: During this timeframe, the company rolled out a new service and selling program. The initiative inspired our entire team to step outside their comfort zone to grow the level of service we provided, so we built on "DA SQUAD" and continued to focus on their leadership development.

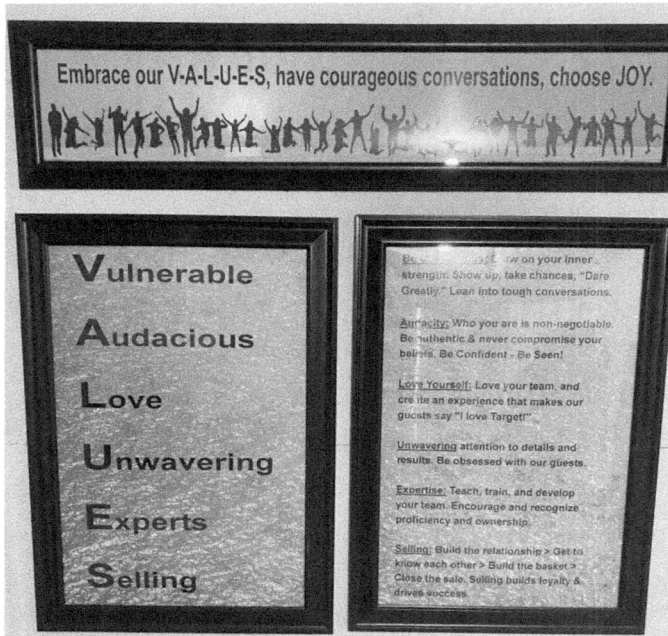

Embrace our V·A·L·U·E·S, have courageous conversations, choose JOY.

Vulnerable

Audacious

Love

Unwavering

Experts

Selling

Be Vulnerable: Draw on your inner strength. Show up, take chances, "Dare Greatly." Lean into tough conversations.

Audacity: Who you are is non-negotiable. Be authentic & never compromise your beliefs. Be Confident - Be Seen!

Love Yourself: Love your team, and create an experience that makes our guests say "I love Target!"

Unwavering attention to details and results. Be obsessed with our guests.

Expertise: Teach, train, and develop your team. Encourage and recognize proficiency and ownership.

Selling: Build the relationship > Get to know each other > Build the basket > Close the sale. Selling builds loyalty & drives success.

The silhouettes are all the leaders on my team, including me, "jumping for joy," which was super fun! A key person on my team was responsible for bringing these to life and was one of my creative partners for many years. Thank you, Kiley Sarazin! What an amazing, talented person.

These are related to the retail business and may not make sense to you and your team, but my purpose in sharing them is merely to offer some examples. We would create a poster for each new acronym and display it in visible areas, and all would refer to it frequently to help keep the team aware and focused on our mission. Any one-on-one status time would include a check-in on each point. It ended up being a vital tool to help the team focus on our goals.

Using acronyms isn't essential, but the point is to ensure you're doing something to keep your team focused on the mission, make your messaging fresh, and ensure your folks are engaged and energized in their roles.

Companies often use the same idea to draw attention to their business. They frequently use "tag-lines" or even the company name to garner interest and pride from their employees and prospective customers. Three examples that I encountered on my walks that jumped out at me were: 1) a moving company entitled Honest and True Moving Crew, 2) an electrical company entitled ABC Electric (**A**biding and **B**elieving in **C**hrist Jesus), and 3) a childcare business entitled Diana's Country Kids, which included the phrase, "An educational ride from your hats to your boots." Catchy and easy to remember. Would you be more likely to hire any of these companies if needed? Simple things, in this case titles or phrases, get noticed and can change behavior. The same thing will work with your team. It can help all employees align on a mission or behavior.

Re-Frame, Refocus, Reset

Everyone and every team gets stuck in a rut, loses focus, or loses urgency for the task. Your role as a leader is to snap your folks out of it.

If you wear glasses, you've likely updated your prescription after your vision changed. It feels like a whole new world—everything is clearer with your new lenses, and you no longer get tired when you read. That's the same sort of check-up that individuals on your team inevitably need on occasion.

In addition to a "new prescription," you may need "new frames." I always had similar brown frames and decided to change to the clear frames I have today. I started noticing people viewing me differently. For a couple of weeks after the change in frames, I encountered people who didn't recognize me until I spoke. On one occasion, an HQ partner I had spent several hours with the previous day made eye contact with me as I approached, yet it took him a bit to "see me." A leader's role is to keep the team focused *and* inspired. More than just fresh lenses are sometimes necessary. Occasionally, bright blue or red frames may be the best way to refocus your team.

I once heard a story about a famous and very successful college basketball coach who, in addition to winning numerous national championships, was known for always being in control on the bench and rarely having technical fouls called on himself. It was late in one of those championship games when the team lost focus, and he knew he needed to do something. He decided he wanted to get a technical foul, so he called a timeout and went to talk to the referee, who, after some discussion, did call the technical. When the coach returned to the huddle, he told his team he didn't do anything wrong. His team reacted as he hoped—refocused—and won the game. Resetting and refocusing your team is necessary sometimes, and it is important not to hesitate when the time comes.

Change Your Patterns

I've worked with numerous highly skilled leaders. Some of them could get their messages across ninety five percent of the time by communicating clearly, and they rarely needed to raise their voice or use different strategies. One in particular never showed anger, frustration, or any change in emotion when speaking. As a result, when he tried to give tough messages, they often weren't received with the urgency needed. I encouraged him to let the people who "needed to hear his message differently" assemble in his office for a few minutes before he entered the room. As he entered, I suggested closing the door firmly and looking at each person directly when they turned toward the sound of the door slamming. That minor adjustment and the accompanying body language made the difference for him primarily because it was out of his routine. Interestingly, he mentioned that the tactic still worked for him years later.

It will serve you well if you find a way to make a noticeable change in your patterns to add emphasis. Before an important meeting or presentation, I prepared the meeting room well in advance and assigned a key person to ensure everyone was present. My door was always open, and when the team saw it closed before one of those larger meetings, they knew that I was going to communicate something particularly important.

Regardless of what you decide to do to shake things up to reignite your team, the critical thing is that you see the need to do something and do it in a timely fashion.

> Don't hesitate to change your patterns or shake things up when your team needs to refocus.

Always Be "On" as a Leader

You've likely heard the phrase, "As the leader goes, so goes the team." Have you experienced working for a boss who occasionally showed up somewhat down, cranky, or distracted and noticed its resulting impact on the team? Like most people, you steer clear of that leader in those situations. We all have bad days, but as a leader, it's crucial to understand the negative ramifications when you're off your game to those around you.

Always make it your goal to bring your best self to the job each day and encourage your team to do the same. Spend a few minutes in silent thought or say a few prayers of thanksgiving and gratitude to start your day positively. Rely on what works for you, but be quick to adjust as needed. Positive self-talk and affirmations can be great tools in this situation. Repeat one that you like ten times to yourself several times daily and see if you feel any different. Use your commute to work every day to ensure you're in the right mindset, and if you need to refocus during the workday, take a walk or rely on a feedback partner to help you.

Chapter 12
Empathy

With all the uncertainty and upheaval today, empathy is the final ingredient in my recipe for success, and it's likely the most important one. Since we're dealing with more unrest and anxiety as a society, leaders must be extra focused and dig deep to understand their team's changing needs and ensure their goals and plans are aligned. A key component of empathy is being present and listening to understand the feelings and experiences of others better. It's important to withhold judgment and connect emotionally.

Understanding and Empathy (FFF)

One of Target's signature taglines was Fast-Fun-and-Friendly, and, in support of that, the leaders on my team were trying to acknowledge employees doing things right, etc. If a team member had an opportunity to improve in that area, the supervisor had one-on-one conversations to inspire positive change. One of my new leaders shared one of those conversations. Ellen was a cashier—a pleasant, quiet lady of around seventy years old. She never missed a shift, even though she had to rely on public transportation to get back and forth to work every day. Her leaders had repeatedly reminded and encouraged her about being FFF with no noticeable change, so one of them sat down to discuss it with her. The conversation started with positive reinforcement about her dependability.

When asked why she didn't seem happy at work, Ellen calmly walked her leader through her "normal day" and some of the things going on in her life. Ellen shared that coming to work every day was the best part of her day. The two spent over an hour getting to know and understand each other better. Following that conversation, the leader stopped by my office to share the story with tears in her eyes. We both agreed that if our situation were like Ellen's, we likely wouldn't get out of bed in the morning. Her daily challenges and difficulties were more than most people could handle. From that day forward, we all tried to brighten her day and appreciate her differently. That lesson reminded me of the importance of connecting and building a foundational relationship at all levels of leadership.

There's much information about empathy today, and I encourage you to learn more about it. Brené Brown's short video on this subject is a great starting point.

Where are you on "the empathy scale" today? Is it a natural thing for you? How often do you think about the needs of others? It's good to remember that empathy is a skill and something we can train ourselves to improve on if we consciously practice it. Know that if you have a growth mindset and continuous learning approach, and empathy is a part of your skillset, this is your ***time to shine*** as a leader!

Notes and Thoughts:

Section Five
Never Stop Learning
The Rest of the Story

"In times like these, it helps to recall that there have always been times like these."

— Paul Harvey

Chapter 13
Persistence

Several additional areas can impact your path to leadership success, and each could fill a book on its own.

Even with a detailed plan, your path to success will encounter numerous roadblocks and you'll need the fortitude to power through. There will be surprises and difficulties, so expect them and quickly eliminate them. You must have a desire and positive approach that's strong enough to handle whatever comes up on your path to success.

While I was in an HQ role and trying to sell my boss on a new presentation initiative, I wouldn't always get the desired response and would be sent back to the drawing board. Knowing I felt strongly about it, I would regroup with my team, take another look at the plan, and re-present it for approval. I clearly remember one of the situations when the project content stayed virtually the same, with a few minor changes to make the presentation more straightforward. He loved it and presented it to the CEO, who approved it. When I pointed out that it was virtually the same plan I showed earlier, he acknowledged it but said he wanted to understand better how strongly I felt about it. That lesson in persistence stuck with me.

A recent example of persistence and true grit is NFL quarterback Alex Smith. He had already survived many challenges in his career but had a strong desire to realize his dream of again playing the sport he loves. In 2018, he suffered a horrible injury that nearly cost him his leg and, at one point, threatened his life due to a severe infection. He endured more than a dozen surgeries spanning almost two years, during which he repeatedly played out his return in his head. He believed he would make it back. He encountered endless mental and physical challenges throughout his recovery and navigated those challenges with the support of his family and friends, plus unwavering persistence and perseverance. He was voted NFL Comeback Player of the Year in 2020.

Most of us won't have to overcome such a significant obstacle to find success, but just know that there will be challenges and that if prepared for them, you will overcome them just as Alex Smith did!

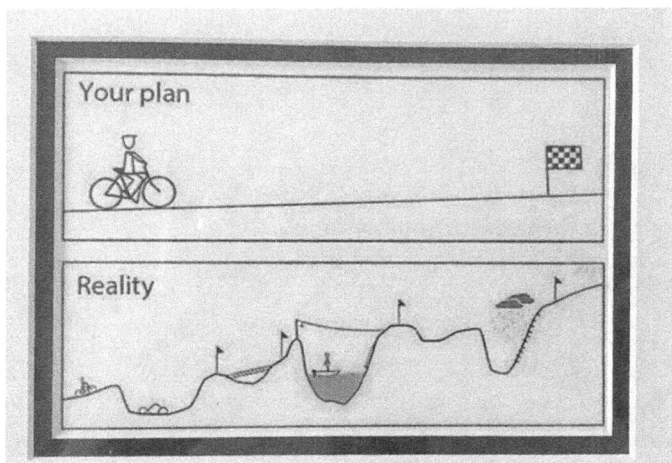

The road to success isn't a straight shot—it will include peaks and valleys, but if you're persistent, you'll prevail. The journey is exciting and beneficial, and it's good to remember that significant growth often happens in the declines and on the plateaus before you climb out of the valleys.

Notes and Thoughts:

Chapter 14
Where Do You Find Your Inspiration?

Have passion, take action, and magic will happen.

I'm always interested to see and hear what inspires people. Some of the most inspiring experiences come from the world of sports. There are many great leadership examples, techniques, and stories, and I wanted to share a few that proved meaningful to me.

Mark, Mona, Mindy, Mickey, Mary, Murray, Meg, Matt

It wasn't until I graduated from college that I learned why my parents decided to name me Murray after the legendary Minnesota Gophers Football coach.

Murray Warmath was the coach for eighteen seasons from 1954 to 1971. My dad was a big fan because of how he approached the game, invested in developing his players (many went on to successful pro careers), and, ultimately, the team's success. My dad was very competitive in sports in his younger years and instilled that competitive spirit in all of his kids, especially me. He engaged differently regarding sports and constantly encouraged me to work harder and practice more. He met me where I was and pushed me beyond where I thought I could go—the same approach I tried to take with the individuals on my teams over the years.

Bill Belichick

The New England Patriots are a true football dynasty under Coach Bill Belichick. He expects excellence from his players and coaches. He's laser-focused on preparation for each game and puts together a precise game plan that attacks the opponents' weaknesses. In addition, he encourages the same from his players, having them prepare for the players they line up against on the line of scrimmage. Details make the difference in his approach, evidenced by his numerous Super Bowl wins. Bill Belichick is a leader—a genius at bringing out the best in others and helping people feel like they belong. He has exceptionally high standards for himself and those around him. He's a great coach and leader, and he is a winner. Sure, he had Tom Brady, and the combination of the two of them clearly helped, but one man doesn't win championships, teams do.

Olympic Gold

In 1980, when I was in college, I remember the anticipation and excitement around the upcoming Lake Placid Winter Olympics—so much so that I bought a new TV just for the occasion. You've likely seen Gavin O'Connor's *Miracle,* about Team USA beating the Russians in the Olympics and then winning the gold medal. Coach Herb Brooks selected the players and assembled the team, consisting of the best college players from several teams, plus a few others. He had to mold a bunch of kids into a team that would take on the best teams in the world. Herb employed "tough love" and several other tactics to build mental focus and physical resiliency in his players and to bring them together. As a result, he led that team of young college players to accomplish an astonishing feat.

Their preparation included a sixty one-game pre-

Olympic schedule. Interestingly, just a week before in the last prep game, the US team played the Russians in a "Friendly," and were embarrassed ten to three. A couple of weeks later, when they faced the Russians again, it was an incredible and memorable game—this time in the Olympics. It was so inspiring to see this team play their best game together on a worldwide stage. It's something I'll never forget. Leadership and coaching made all the difference. The Team USA's accomplishment and story are an incredible example of exceptional leadership and coaching by Herb Brooks. It's worth a read and watch if it interests you.[1]

John Wooden

There aren't many people like the legendary John Wooden. People like to talk about his esteemed coaching career, but one thing about his coaching style that often flies under the radar is how he prepared his teams. It was unlike virtually every other coach. He never prepared for an opponent. Instead, all his focus and energy went to his team playing their best and executing the details of their plays and strategies. Excellence in detail also defined his genius. He believed that if his players played their best together, they would be hard to beat. He was right and, as a result, established a record of success at UCLA that will likely never be beaten in college sports.

Apollos Hester

Have you heard of Apollos Hester? In 2014, he was a high school football player and was interviewed by the local news about his team after a big win. It was simply incredible and something I've shared with my teams (and kids) numerous times over the years. It demonstrated the importance of attitude, hard work, believing in your success, never giving up on your dreams, and finishing strong in two minutes and twenty nine seconds. Who doesn't have two minutes to be inspired? I encourage you to check him out on YouTube.[2]

Susan Boyle

There are plenty of inspirational examples outside of sports. One of my all-time favorites is Susan Boyle. In 2009, a somewhat awkward forty seven-year-old woman took the stage at *Britain's Got Talent* and shocked the world. You've likely seen it—the audition has some twenty five million views.[3] It's one of a kind and still sends shivers down my back. The moral of her story is to never judge a book by its cover. No one would have predicted that this woman, who suffers from Asperger's Syndrome, would have such incredible talent. She credits hard work and years of practice in her church for giving her the confidence to sign up for the competition. Hard work, constant training, refining the basic skills . . . sound familiar?

Remember, as a leader, sharing what inspires you reveals more about yourself which will positively impact your team.

My Inspiration

It's hard to narrow down exactly where I've found the most inspiration in my life and career. It indeed comes from the people in my life, the books I read, the success stories of others, and so much more. If you're like me, you take your foundation for granted and often the people.

However, my parents and family are my foundation, and it's growing stronger every day. Take the time today to let those who created the meaningful moments in your life know how much you appreciate them. Reflect on who and what has fueled your success and inspired you so far. Be grateful for those moments and remember to pay them forward.

For many years in the Minneapolis area, a daily

column in the local newspaper featured articles by extraordinarily talented and successful people like Dale Dauten, Stephen Wilbers, and numerous others. Harvey Mackay, a seven-time *New York Times* best-selling author and successful business-man, frequently contributed with his column enti-tled "Outswimming The Sharks." I've read dozens of his articles over the years and kept many that my mom clipped out. She knew what inspired me, wanted the best for me, and continued to encourage me throughout her entire life. She sent me envelopes full of business articles every few weeks until she was well into her eighties. She was and is a massive inspi-ration, and I still feel her presence. Thanks, Mom!

Shortly after she passed, my sister found three classic "cut-outs" that my mom had saved. I think they give a small glimpse of this remarkable woman. We are truly blessed that she was our mom.

A Prayer for Older People - William Strawn

Father, thou knowest I am growing older. Keep me from becoming talkative and possessed with the idea that I must express myself on every subject. Release me from the craving to straighten out everyone's affairs. Keep my mind free from the recital of endless detail. Seal my lips when I am inclined to tell of my aches and pains. Teach me the glorious lesson that occa-sionally I may be wrong. Make me thoughtful but not moody, helpful but not bossy. With my vast store of wisdom and experi-ence, it seems a pity not to use it all, but thou knowest, Lord, that I want to keep my friends until the end. Amen.

John Westphal

amily affair

Special garden

Dear Readers: I recently ran across these clever instructions for planting a special garden and couldn't resist sharing them:

First, plant five rows of peas: Preparedness, Promptness, Perseverance, Politeness and Prayer.

Next to them, plant three rows of squash: Squash Gossip, Squash Criticism and Squash Indifference.

Then five rows of lettuce: Let Us Be Faithful, Let Us Be Unselfish, Let Us Be Loyal, Let Us Be Truthful, Let Us Love One Another.

And no garden is complete without turnips: Turn Up for Church, Turn Up With a Smile, Turn Up With Determination.

lum-

What Went Wrong?

This is the story of four working people: Everybody, Somebody, Anybody and Nobody. There was an important job to be done, and Everybody was sure that Somebody would do it. Anybody could have done it, but Nobody did it. Somebody got angry because it was Everybody's job. Everybody thought that Somebody would do it. But Nobody asked Anybody. It ended up that the job wasn't done, and Everybody blamed Somebody, when actually, Nobody asked Anybody.

Whatever it is, find your inspiration and passion and feed it constantly throughout your life. It's a true gift, so be grateful that you found it and share it freely with others. They will never forget it, nor will you.

"Somehow, we've come to believe that greatness is only for the chosen few—for the superstars. The truth is, greatness is for us all. This is not about

lowering expectations but raising them for every last one of us. Greatness is not in one special place, nor in one special person. Greatness is wherever somebody is trying to find it. Find your greatness."

— Unknown Author

Looking Ahead

I shared that one of my goals was to encourage you to believe that *everything you need to find success is already within you*—you just need to recognize, refine, and grow it. What does that success look like to you? Understanding that everyone defines success in a way that's personal to them, psychologists tell us that even the most "successful" among us are likely only accessing fifty to sixty percent of their capabilities. In other words, most of us have much more untapped potential to realize. Are you interested in more fully tapping into your potential?

Exploring that untapped potential, our potential, is the topic of my next book, *Your Perfect is Good Enough*—a work in progress.

Thanks again for your confidence in me and for allowing me to share my journey this way! To all who provided those incredible moments in my life and career, including the countless folks I've not yet written about—THANK YOU! Your impact and inspiration made me who I am today, and I am forever grateful.

Until next time . . .

Notes and Thoughts:

Afterword

As I left Target, I really didn't know what retirement was going to look like, but I knew I wanted to write a book. It's been interesting: three years, Coronavirus, a move to Florida, thousands of miles walked, forty pounds lost, seven pairs of tennis shoes, and many books consumed. You can often find me in the hot tub following one of my daily walks, living my best life.

Throughout my career, I looked for unexpected things that I could do or share to inspire others. It was about making memories and helping others. I've learned that my Target friendships are lifelong, full-circle relationships and we're still creating new memories today, both in Florida and Minnesota.

My last day, the day of my retirement celebration, was a Friday in late January . . . in Minnesota.

Yup, you guessed it, there was a major blizzard! Many people couldn't make it that day due to the storm which was understandable. It did enable me to have more meaningful conversations with those that attended, and that was wonderful.

Another unexpected blessing was the notes and emails I received. As I read them, back then and again now as I wrap up this book, it's clear to me how fortunate I am that our paths crossed. The three I included at the beginning represent different points in my career. I'm so thankful!

Acknowledgments

I'm so fortunate and blessed by so many opportunities and experiences in my life but none more important than the people.

Kiley Sarazin: You, my friend, are incredible! Thank you for your thoughtful feedback and guidance on this book. I so value your perspective. Thanks, too, for making me a better leader and person throughout our time together at Target!

Maureen Berendes, Jeremy Vandeberg, Sondra, and Sam Wash: Thanks for sharing your thoughts and ideas as they were invaluable. I really appreciate it!

Melinda Pederson and Meg Leszko: There is nothing like honest feedback from family. You were a key part of making me the person I am growing up, and I feel so blessed that you impacted this book! I love you!

THANK YOU!!

References

Introduction

1. Brené Brown, PhD, MSW, "Dare to Lead Hub," Brené Brown, https://brenebrown.com/hubs/dare-to-lead/.

3. Laughter

1. TED-Ed. "Everyday Leadership - Drew Dudley," YouTube, 2013. https://www.youtube.com/watch?v=uAy6EawKKME.

2. Stephen C. Lundin, Ph.D., Harry Paul, and John Christensen, *FISH! A Proven Way to Boost Morale and Improve Results* (New York: Hachette, 2000).

5. Optimism

1. Charles Swindoll, "Charles Swindoll Quotes," Goodreads, accessed May 25, 2023, https://www.goodreads.com/quotes/267482-the-longer-i-live-the-more-i-realize-the-impact.

2. Rosenthal, Robert, and Lenore Jacobson, *Pygmalion in the Classroom: Teacher Expectation and Pupils' Intellectual Development.* (New York: Holt, Rinehart and Winston, 1968).

7. Openness

1. "The HBDI (Herrmann Brain Dominance Instrument)" Herrmann, accessed May 24, 2023, https://www.thinkher rmann.com/hbdi.

8. Vulnerability

1. John Eades, "Simple Beliefs Most Managers Reject, But Leaders Embrace," LinkedIn, August 5, 2022, https://www. linkedin.com/pulse/simple-beliefs-most-managers-reject-leaders-embrace-john-eades/?trk=pulse-article_more-arti cles_related-content-card.
2. Theodore Roosevelt, "Citizenship in a Republic" (speech, Paris, April 23, 1910) Theodore Roosevelt Center, https:// www.theodorerooseveltcenter.org/Learn-About-TR/TR-Encyclopedia/Culture-and-Society/Man-in-the-Arena.aspx.

14. Where Do You Find Your Inspiration?

1. O'Connor, Gavin, dir. *Miracle.* (United States: Walt Disney Pictures, Mayhem Pictures, 2004).
2. Mickler, Lauren. "TWC News Austin: High School Blitz Interview with Apollos Hester," Youtube, 2014. https:// www.youtube.com/watch?v=X7ymriMhojo.
3. Britain's Got Talent. "Susan Boyle's First Audition 'I Dreamed a Dream' | Britain's Got Talent," YouTube, 2019. https://www.youtube.com/watch?v=yE1Lxw5ZyXk.